"*His Word Alone* is like sitting d [...] friend. Summer's passion for Goc [...] taking into account the very real struggle we often face with being intimidated or overwhelmed by it. Is God's word really for *you*, right now, where you're at? 'There comes a time when every good Bible study girl needs to push her Bible studies aside so she can dwell alone in the presence of God and His all-sufficient word.' Summer shows us that while the Bible is gloriously deep, we don't have to be afraid of drowning in it. Get ready for your approach to personal Bible study to go from haphazard to productive, from frustration to renewed passion. Soak up these practical tips and get ready to dive in."

— **Sara Wallace,** Author,
*The Gospel-Centered Mom*

"If you are ready to know God and not just know about Him, pick up this book! In an engaging and transparent way, Summer initiates a conversation every person and church needs to explore. God is speaking to us all the time through his word, but are we really listening?"

— **Brad Hodges,** Discipleship Pastor,
Temple Baptist Church

"I have long respected Summer and her capacity to teach God's word. I was thrilled to see this book—what a timely and necessary call to all of us! This book has the capacity to deeply change us as we fall truly in love with the scriptures."

—**Dr. Peter Swann,** Lead Pastor, Hope Church;
Executive Director, Every Village

"Every believer has been given an appetite for the scriptures, but the magnitude of truth is overwhelming and debilitating for many. Summer Lacy's book *His Word Alone* helps walk women through a living and actual way to learn and love the word of God. I trust Summer enough to entrust her with teaching the scriptures to hundreds of women in our church. I highly respect Summer, and I highly recommend this book of Summer's to you."

—**Jason Shepperd,** Lead Pastor,
Church Project

# His *Word* Alone

A call to put down
your Bible studies and
pick up your Bible

SECOND EDITION

SUMMER LACY

LUCIDBOOKS

**His Word Alone**
A Call to Put Down Your Bible Studies and Pick Up Your Bible
Copyright © 2018 by Summer Lacy
Photography: Angèle Hamilton

Published by Lucid Books in Houston, TX
www.LucidBooksPublishing.com

ISBN-10: 1-63296-202-0  |  ISBN-13: 978-1-63296-202-7
eISBN-10: 1-63296-203-9  |  eISBN-13: 978-1-63296-203-4

For as the rain and the snow come down from heaven
and do not return there but water the earth,
making it bring forth and sprout,
giving seed to the sower and bread to the eater,
so shall my word be that goes out from my mouth;
it shall not return to me empty,
but it shall accomplish that which I purpose,
and shall succeed in the thing for which I sent it.
—Isaiah 55:10–11

*For Chris, who said I would long before I ever knew I could.*
*I'm setting my heart intently on that final Texas sunset,*
*and each and every one the Lord gives us in between.*
*You are my most favorite ever.*

# Table of Contents

# Foreword

It was in the spring that I first met Summer. She is the real deal. Summer is a wife, a mom, a speaker, and a mentor. Most of all, her heart is in the right place. She's not trying to build a name for herself, or become famous. She knows those matters are in God's hands.

When I asked Summer why she was writing a book about the Bible, she said, "I want people to read it." I was stunned, stopped in my tracks. Wow! How simple and profound. Today, the Christian landscape is littered with courses and curricula on how to study the Bible. Summer has hit upon the difficulty we all share when picking up our Bible that the step before studying scripture is first, to read it.

The simple act of reading, that's the strategy. You don't have to be an expert in biblical interpretation, a master of exegesis, or a doctor of theology. You simply take the book, open it, and read. Allowing your eyes to fall across the sacred pages rescues the text from becoming distorted propaganda, mere information, or hard cold facts. Summer reminds us that His word alone is enough.

Summer has launched a revolution of reading scripture with fresh eyes. The reading of scripture creates a profound change in our reality. It taps into the creative sources of faith. It opens up bold thoughts of possibility. It brings about a new compassion for the hurts of others. It opens us up to the help of God's Spirit. And it surprises us with confidence that God is our future.

The way forward lies in reaching back—back to the rich text of scripture, back to the world of God's word. By reading—just reading—we discover God's word. We hear it speaking from the world in which it was written into the world in which we live.

The Bible is a buffet. We are to feed on it. God's word is meant to be taken, tasted, savored, digested, and metabolized into our spirit until it energizes our living. The goal of reading is not to finish a book, but to meet with the God of the Bible. *His Word Alone* is not a book about mastering scripture. It's a book about letting scripture master us.

Summer's role in the journey of helping rediscover a raw, rich, robust, revitalized reading of scripture is not that of an author but of a friend and fellow follower of Jesus. She invites us to think about what it truly means to read scripture. Summer stands alongside us to help keep our feet firmly on the ground of the text as she lifts the heart and mind toward God.

To read—to really read—the Bible, simply and power-fully, we must learn to live in the scriptures, to develop a rhythm of reading and living, letting the chapters and verses have a say in everything we say and do. It's that easy and profound.

Dr. David Edwards
Author, speaker, and Pastor of Discipleship at Church Project in Spring, Texas

# Acknowledgments

Chris, Cole, Jacob, and Joshua. You all have made me so much more than I am. Thank you for bearing the brunt of this whole book-writing business alongside me.

Melanie, Kristina, and Teal. You all are the best contributing editors a girl could ever hope for—not to mention some of the finest friends, snort-inducing conversationalists, cheerleaders, and truth-tellers that I've ever had the honor of walking beside. Thank you for your time, encouragement, and seriousness in helping me get this thing done. You occupy every single page of this book.

Tribe of 12. You listened to everything I never wanted to say. I've learned so very much about God's good grace through you. Such an unbelievable honor to know your stories.

Andrea. Sheesh. Six figures couldn't even begin to repay you for all the ideas, encouragement, and sympathy you've offered me during this endeavor. I'm grateful for you.

Ashley E. You stepped in at the last minute and saved the day. As if I didn't adore you enough already.

Ladies of the Rising (and your fellows, too). You gave me space to learn and grow at the front of that classroom every Sunday morning for years. I fell in love with God's word right before your very eyes. Thank you for giving me room to find my footing and for the many ensuing years of friendship that have followed.

## Introduction
## Put Down Your Bible Studies

I was a Christian for years before I ever read the Bible. That's not to say that I didn't try to read it. I did. I'd start at Genesis 1, planning to read straight through, only to be overcome by discouragement around Genesis 10 (the flood followed by a genealogy = my ruin). I'd turn to the New Testament Gospels and have a much easier time following the storyline, but I'd get lost somewhere in the midst of Jesus's parables. It didn't take long for me to become disheartened.

Seemingly unable to understand the text on my own, I quickly turned to Bible studies to lead me through, to state the things I couldn't discern for myself, and to tell me what I needed to understand about scripture. That proved to be a much easier task than the flat-out reading of the Bible, so I comfortably continued this way for years—one study after another, after another.

In the spring of 2010, my husband volunteered us to begin co-teaching a married young adults Bible class at the church we attended, to which I promptly said no. I may have been a sold-out-to-Bible-study-girl, but I told him there was no way I could *teach* the Bible. I had taught communication studies for years before our home began bursting with babies, so my problem was not with the teaching part. It was with the Bible part. I was suddenly struck by the fact that I didn't know the Bible well enough to teach it.

This realization took me off guard. I had spent years studying the Bible by now, yet I still had no confidence in my ability to understand it on my own. It seemed that my constant reliance on Bible studies had handicapped me in a way I didn't expect. I had become dependent on those who knew the Bible better than I to teach the Bible to me and neglected my responsibility to dig into God's word on my own. I had allowed the Bible study to replace my own study of the Bible.

What's troubling about my dilemma is that it isn't uniquely mine. It plagues an entire generation of Sunday morning churchgoers and Bible study enthusiasts who accessorize their lives with biblical truth instead of clothing themselves in it. This isn't merely a hunch on my part. As I began asking other women about their go-to methods of Bible study, it became clear that many of them were just like I had been: too timid or too unsure of their ability to understand God's word to even attempt studying it on their own.

Through these conversations with other women, I uncovered a whole gaggle of Bible study girls just like me. Like me, many of them were familiar with the stories, characters, and events of the Bible, but they were at a total loss when it came to comprehending the major themes and overall point of the Bible. Like me, they were genuine in their search for more of Christ. Like me, they had spent years "studying" the Bible only to emerge with very little understanding of it. My hope in writing this book is that collectively, we Bible study girls might do something to correct that.

So what's wrong with the Bible study approach to studying scripture? After all, aren't Bible studies a good thing? Don't many of our churches place buffets of Bible studies before us each semester and encourage us to pick, choose, and partake? Right from the start I want to be very clear as to what I'm *not* saying. I'm not saying you need to stop doing Bible studies. I would hate to throw any of you into a full-blown conniption fit right here in the intro. I love a good Bible study. I'm a writer of Bible studies myself. My bookshelves are swelling with studies, commentaries, devotionals, and the like. These materials have played an invaluable role in my growth as a Christ-follower.

- I was first convinced that the Bible was the living, breathing word of God while sitting on the edge of my seat in a jam-packed auditorium as Beth Moore taught from the depths of her soul.

- I first began understanding the Bible as one, unified story while devouring every single Matt Chandler sermon I could fit on my iPod.

- I first saw Jesus saturating the pages of the Old Testament as I poured over a Nancy Guthrie devotional.

- I first realized that every single word in the Bible was profitable as I listened to Jen Wilkin teach on every. single. word. of Genesis, Exodus, and Joshua.

Thank God for these teachers, writers, and speakers of God's truth. Thank God for the books, sermons, and podcasts that amplify His word. The Lord has taught, reproved, corrected, and trained me through such means. No, my goal is not to compel you to do away with such Bible study resources.

However, we can no longer ignore the reality that all too often we substitute them for the Bible itself, snacking on and picking at the word of God instead of greedily consuming it. When our diet of Bible consumption consists mostly of excerpts from scripture given in devotionals, small segments of Bible reading done through Bible studies, and whatever passage the pastor is preaching on at church each week, we miss the opportunity to experience God for ourselves.

To do this, we must dig our own hands down into the grit, grime, and beauty of scripture through systematically reading and studying the Bible *on our own*. Ultimately, my contention is that in our over-reliance on Bible study materials, we have attempted to substitute a person's word about God's word for God's word itself, and we're missing God in the process.

No matter how many times you may have tried and failed to study the Bible on your own, each and every one of us is able and very capable of studying the Bible this way. More than that, we have each been called to it.

> *Do your best to present yourself to God as one approved, a worker who has no need to be ashamed, rightly handling the word of truth.*
>
> —2 Timothy 2:15

In the pages that follow, I will explore the Bible study dilemma by asking you the same tough questions I asked my sold-out-to-Bible-study self over the course of these last several years:

- Have you consistently chosen Bible studies (a person's word about God's word) over the Bible (God's word itself)?

- Do you trust your Bible teachers and pastors to guide you through the Bible to the exclusion of the Holy Spirit's work to do the same?

❧ Do you skip past the words of scripture in order to get to the understanding and application of those very words?

If, like me, you've answered those questions with a resounding yes, this book is for you.

In Part I, we're going to examine the problem and identify the reasons behind it as we seek to answer the question, "Why are we more prone to pick up a Bible study than the Bible itself?" In Part II, we'll turn our attention to a solution as together we learn how to successfully dive into scripture on our own (and I think you'll find the process surprisingly simple).

When we do this, when we dare to take the responsibility of Bible study into our very own hands, we acknowledge the Bible to be completely unique and *sufficient unto itself* as God's living word. That realization is a complete game-changer. By the end of this book, I want you to know this to be true so deep down in your bones that you'll actually pick up your Bible and read.

The reason I am so passionate about the serious, individual study of God's word by Christians is because it is the very means through which the Lord has claimed my heart and transformed my life. His word has met me right where I was at the time, no matter where or when. It has relentlessly pursued me through the hard work of marriage, the endless delights and difficulties of raising small children, every insecurity and uncertainty a 30-something-stay-at-home mom could muster, and all the other ups, downs, ins, and outs of everyday life. There is no pain to which His word does not speak, no joy that it does not birth.

If God speaks to me in this powerful of a manner through His word, He can speak to you in this very same way, too.

It is my desperate desire that all women would come to know the power of His word as they commit themselves wholeheartedly to the study of it. Ladies, the Bible is enough! His word alone is all we need. There comes a time when every good Bible study girl needs to push her Bible studies aside so she can dwell alone in the presence of God and His all-sufficient word.

When you do this, I assure you, your own Bible study will be the most fruitful Bible study of all.

# Part I

# The Thing about Bible Studies

# Chapter 1: The Bible Study Girl's Dilemma

*Seek from the book of the LORD, and read.*
—Isaiah 34:16 NASB

From junior high on, I remember everyone being pretty much defined by what they were into, or good at doing. The problem I very quickly ran into after walking across the threshold of Bailey Jr. High School in Arlington, Texas, was that I had no idea what this was for me. What was I into? What was *I* good at doing? And perhaps most importantly at the time, where did I fit in?

First, you had the much-coveted athletes—the cheerleaders, the soccer and football players, the track and field competitors, and so on. That was not my thing. I tried to make it my thing, even going so far as to try out for the girls' basketball team in seventh grade. I didn't even make the D-team cut. My husband has since told me that that was a very hard thing to do. Okay, so obviously not my thing.

Then there were the musicians—the band kids, the choir, the orchestra, the drumline. I tried my hand at music as well, but my talent got me about as far as the fifth grade recorder. Play with me now: "Hot cross buns, hot cross buns. One-a-penny, two-a-penny, hoooottttt crooooooossss buuuuuunnnnnnssssss!" Too bad gusto doesn't compensate for tone deafness. I'm pretty sure those sour notes still haunt my mother's dreams. Okay, so most definitely not my thing.

Then you had the smart kids—honor roll, honor society, science club, Latin club, math club. While I did well in school and always enjoyed learning and studying, I never had the desire to pursue academics with the rigor that these kids did. Okay, so maybe not my thing.

I floundered around without a group to call my own until I walked into Mrs. Gardner's eighth grade speech class in the fall of 1992. I quickly became enamored with all things speech—the writing, the performance, the expression of ideas, the clarity of communication. But even more significant, my 13-year-old self fit in here. I liked the people, and, praise the good Lord in heaven, it seemed as if they liked me, too (spiral perm and all). I had found my place and quickly proclaimed speech as "my thing."

It remained my thing throughout the rest of junior high, into high school, and right through to college. I loved it and worked incredibly hard at it. But here's the thing: I honestly wasn't all that good at it. Sure, I had some success here and there, but overall, I simply did not have the natural inclination to excel in that realm like some of my peers so obviously did. I would put in all the time and effort that my little heart could muster and yet still fall short at competition. I was constantly working yet rarely advancing. It was beyond discouraging. It was downright disheartening. All the end-of-the-year most-improved and most-dedicated awards did little to console me. How on earth could I work so hard at something and remain so mediocre? (Now before you feel too sorry for me, I turned out just fine and have learned that losing often carries far greater lessons than winning.)

## On Feelings of Defeat

While the shelves in my study remain conspicuously absent of any speech trophies I pined for back then, those many years of speech classes, coaching, competitions, and all the persistent trying and failing taught me to recognize a feeling I would meet up with much later, in the most unexpected of places: Christianity.

Something you ought to know about me right off the bat is that I'm not the type of girl who gives 10%. When I'm in, I'm *all* in. So when I became a Christian in my early 20s, I immediately entered into the religion with the feeling that I had a lot of catching up to do. I was pretty much 20 years behind at that point. I wasn't raised in church, never once attended vacation Bible school or a Sunday service, and even though I owned several Bibles, (born and raised in the Bible Belt, y'all), I had no idea what to do with them. I wasn't even going to make the Christian D-team at this rate, so I quickly got to work.

It seemed obvious to me that the first thing I needed to tackle was the Bible. I sat down, began to read, and immediately failed quite miserably. This book was huge. And old. And I'm going to lower my voice to a whisper for this next part—boring. There had to be another way. Seriously, was there a CliffsNotes for the Bible or something? (There actually is, by the way, but I forbid you to go there.)

I clearly could not understand this text on my own, and being too prideful to resort to the actual CliffsNotes version, I decided to go another route: a Bible study. It seemed like the perfect solution. Bible studies were abundant and very much encouraged in church. And they made so much more sense than the Bible itself. A-ha! I had finally found a way to circumvent reading the Bible and yet still remain a Christ-following Christian (read as sarcasm). I became a Bible study enthusiast and remained that way for years. One study at a time, I was going to figure this thing out.

Yet despite my initial enthusiasm and determined commitment, after several years of Bible study efforts, I came out from beneath the pile of studies I had been working through, exhausted. I took a deep breath and realized how very much I was found lacking. All those years after my speech competition days ended, those very same feelings of defeat—of putting so much effort in but reaping so little reward—reappeared after consuming hundreds of pages of dozens of Bible studies.

Despite my concerted attempts to absolutely nail Christianity, I still somehow felt as if I were failing, missing something, or not getting the greater point. What was I doing wrong? Was it possible to be "not good" at the Bible? Could I fail at understanding scripture like I had failed at other things in my life? And most significantly, could I honestly seek knowledge of God and still come out wanting?

I felt completely and utterly defeated. I had been Bible studying my little heart out. I had read so much about who Christ is and what He does. I had learned about the history, the stories, the events, and the people of the Bible. I had seen first hand the effects the Bible had on the women around me who loved it and pursued an understanding of it as I sat in those Bible study classrooms. Yet somehow, I still could not identify those same outcomes in myself. Why not? I was frustrated, exhausted, and overwhelmed by the amount of effort I had put into this thing, only to emerge with so much knowledge but so little benefit.

And then it finally dawned on me that I had not actually been studying the Bible.

I had been studying *about* the Bible. Around it. Picking through bits and pieces of it. Seriously considering the insights that other people had about it. It's not that I hadn't learned, or come to understand, or even experienced so many good, right, and true things during those years. Not at all. But it was as if I had been furiously collecting puzzle pieces only to realize that I had long ago thrown away the picture on the box. I had allowed Bible studies to replace *my own* Bible study. And I was missing God because of it.

## A Good Hair to Split

Perhaps you think I'm splitting hairs here. And that's a fair point to make. After all, in doing Bible studies, aren't we studying the Bible? Does it really make that much of a difference?

Well, that depends, at least in part, on how you use the Bible study. Perhaps you're already using Bible studies correctly, as supplemental to your study of God's word instead of in exclusion to your study of God's word. If so, good for you! You've hit the mark, and that's where we all want to be: using Bible studies as occasional supplements but the Bible itself for daily sustenance.

But for the most part, I was *not* using Bible studies in this way, and I have a suspicion that neither are some of you. I was dependent on them—absolutely uninterested in engaging God's word without a Bible-study mediator (or a pastor or a teacher). Those things created a comfortable buffer between me and God's word. It created more space and wiggle room than He wanted between Him and me.

There is a significant difference between someone telling you what God's word says and listening to what He is saying on your own. In the first instance, someone is relaying to you who God is and what He is like—the things He does and what He desires. In the latter, you are meeting with God to discover those things yourself. So yes, I believe it does make a difference. And if I'm splitting a hair here, it's a good hair to split.

## Why It Matters

Since the fall of man in Genesis 3, we humans have needed a mediator between God and us. Prior to the fall, Adam and Eve walked with God in unhindered fellowship and didn't need a mediator. Genesis 2:25 describes our original condition as naked and not ashamed. (I.cannot.even.fathom.) Once sin entered the world through Adam and Eve's rebellion, their relationship with God was fractured. Sin created a rift, a gaping chasm, a huge gulf between God and people.

Before you go getting all high and mighty on Adam and Eve, remember that at some point or another, each and every one of us has made the same decision they made in that garden. We've disobeyed God. Turned away from Him. Followed our own desires. They may have gone first, but we willingly jumped in after. This distance between God and us made it necessary for a go-between or an intermediary to step in and mediate. Throughout the Bible, we are reminded of our very great need for this mediator.

In the Old Testament, men such as Moses filled this role. The Israelites unabashedly realized their need for an intermediary. Take a look at God giving the Ten Commandments:

> Now when all the people saw the thunder and the flashes of lightning and the sound of the trumpet and the mountain smoking, the people were afraid and trembled, and they stood far off and said to Moses, "You speak to us, and we will listen; but do not let God speak to us, lest we die." Moses said to the people,

*"Do not fear, for God has come to test you, that the fear of him may be before you, that you may not sin." The people stood far off, while Moses drew near to the thick darkness where God was.*

—Exodus 20:18–21

God didn't simply hand over the law to the Israelites; He gave the law to Moses to give to the Israelites. Moses was the mediator between God and the Israelites, and they recognized him as such. As the history of the Old Testament progresses, we see mediators in different forms: judges, kings, prophets, priests. Different people and titles, they all held the same role—to stand in the gap between God and people. To communicate His word to them. To raise up their pleas to Him on their behalf.

These Old Testament mediators foreshadowed Jesus— the better judge, the King of Kings, the ultimate prophet, the great high priest—the one who would "once and for all" close the gap between God and humans through the sacrifice of His own life (Heb. 10:10). In so doing, He became the last and only mediator we would ever need.

*For there is one God, and there is one mediator between God and men, the man Christ Jesus.*

—1 Timothy 2:5

We need no other intermediary. We need no one else to stand between God and us—to communicate to us on His behalf or to raise up our pleas to Him. This is the work Jesus accomplished.

But old habits die hard.

Over the course of church history, battles have been fought, lines have been drawn, and entire people groups have separated over this very issue. Should everyone have intimate, unfettered access to God, or do we still need a mediator other than Christ? This has played out largely in the extent to which God's word, the Bible, has been made available to the masses. The question has always been this: Should only the learned, trained, and rightly educated be allowed access to the Bible, those who can then interpret and relay it to us lay people?

Men such as John Wycliffe, an Oxford professor, scholar, and theologian in the 1300s, believed this to be a dangerous line of thinking and completely contrary to biblical teaching, allowing for corruption and abuse of power within the church. He led an effort to get the Bible into the hands of the masses in their own native languages after 700 years of the text being available only in Latin, the language of an elite few.

After Wycliffe came a long line of people dedicated to their belief that God meant His word to be in our hands. Martin Luther, Erasmus, and William Tyndale were just a few. This is a very abridged version of a long and complicated history, but the point I want to make here is that the Bible sitting on your kitchen table is there because people refused to bow down to the notion that God's word should only be available to some. It was a battle hard fought, with droves of casualties.

Jesus lived and died so we would need no other mediator. These people lived and died so we could read God's good news of salvation directly and with unhindered access.

Have we, with our over-reliance on Bible studies, teachers, pastors, academics, and theologians, given this access away? Have we backed away from the Bible ourselves and put it back in the hands of only the learned, trained, and rightly educated? And in doing so, have we lost much of what God intended us to have? Have we forfeited the direct access God has given us to Him through His word?

Here is why it matters.

It matters because I have no doubt that those of you reading these words have genuine hearts for Christ. You are actively looking for more of Him. You are Bible-studying your little hearts out. You are working hard but still feeling as if you're missing out. You are striving for and grasping at the very great promises God has given, all the while unwittingly circumventing the means through which He has intended to give them: His word.

This is every Bible study girl's dilemma, and it's time for us to wise up. So girls, get out your Bibles. In chapter 2, I want you to see for yourself something utterly astounding about our God.

## Chapter 1: Dig in Deeper
Questions for Study and Reflection
(Copies of worksheets are available at https://www.hiswordalone.com/book)

1. Look up the following verses. Write them out in the space provided.

   ❧ Deuteronomy 8:3

   ❧ Deuteronomy 32:45–47

2. Using these verses, list some things God wants us to know about His word.

3. What do these verses assure us that God's word will do for us?

4. What do these verses instruct us to do with God's word?

## Chapter 2: God Speaks (To you. Right now.)

*Call to me and I will answer you, and will tell you
great and hidden things that you have not known.*
— Jeremiah 33:3

The Old Testament tells us the story of God calling out
to a young boy in the middle of the night. The boy's name
was Samuel, and he would go on to become a great teacher,
judge, and prophet to Israel.

Samuel began serving the Lord under the direction of Eli,
the priest. Eli was an old man at this point, hard of hearing
and dim of sight. Late one night, Samuel and Eli were both
resting at the temple when the Lord called out to the boy,
"Samuel!" (1 Sam. 3:6).

The Lord's voice was so clear and distinct that Samuel
jumped right out of bed and ran to Eli, assuming that Eli
was the one who called out to him. (After all, who walks
around actually expecting to hear God speak?) Samuel was
puzzled when Eli replied something like this: "Nope, wasn't
me." Samuel returned to bed, believing he must have been
mistaken.

The exact same scene played itself out two more times
before Eli finally realized that maybe the boy wasn't
hallucinating. Maybe the Lord was calling out to Samuel.
Eli raised this possibility with Samuel. And once Samuel

recognized the voice of the Lord for what it was, he was faithful to attend to it.

God called out to Samuel once again, and this time, correctly understanding who was speaking to him, Samuel responded, "Speak, for your servant hears" (1 Sam. 3:10). God did speak to Samuel that night, and He continued to speak to him in the years that followed. 1 Samuel 3:19 tells us that God was with Samuel as he grew and that He "let none of his words fall to the ground." God faithfully brought to pass everything that He spoke, and the boy heard.

## God's Word, Spoken

God's voice rang out as clear as a bell to Samuel that night long ago. But that wasn't the first time God spoke to someone, and it wouldn't be the last. In fact, God began speaking to His creation the very moment He created us. Adam was only seconds out of the dust of the ground when God began guiding, directing, and interacting with him. Go back to that first chapter of Genesis with me.

> So God created man in his own image, in the image of God he created him; male and female he created them. And God blessed them. And God said to them, "Be fruitful and multiply and fill the earth and subdue it, and have dominion over the fish of the sea and over the birds of the heavens and over every living thing that moves on the earth."
>
> —Genesis 1:27–28

This communicative relationship between God and His creation can be seen all throughout the Old Testament. As you flip through the pages of the Old Testament from Genesis to Malachi, you will see words such as these repeated again and again: then God *said* (Gen. 8:15), God *spoke* to Israel

(Gen. 46:2), thus *says* the Lord (Jer. 30:2), the God of Israel *has spoken* (2 Sam. 23:3).

I had read all those words and taken in all those stories without even batting an eye. I had flown right past the marvel of God speaking to people so many times that I had given myself whiplash. And then, for some reason, the truth of it stopped me cold when I set out to study about a woman named Hagar.

We meet up with this minor biblical character smack dab in the middle of Abraham's story in Genesis 16. If you're at all familiar with Abraham, you might remember that God made him a few promises. You know, tiny things like "in your offspring shall all the nations of the earth be blessed" (Gen. 22:18).

But the tiny problem with God's big ol' promises to Abraham was that Sarah, Abraham's wife, was barren. Since Sarah and Abraham couldn't see a way around their little predicament of needing an heir but having none, they decided to go rogue and figure things out on their own.

That's when Sarah comes up with a real zinger of an idea: *Here, honey, take my Egyptian maidservant, Hagar, and conceive a child by her.* As you might have guessed, this is where things go bad. Hagar does, indeed, conceive a child by Abraham, cops a bit of an attitude about it with her mistress (mind you, this is from Sarah's perspective), and that's all it takes for Sarah to lose it. She and Abraham have the marital blowout of the century.

> *And Sarai said to Abram, "May the wrong done to me be on you! I gave my servant to your embrace, and when she saw that she had conceived, she looked on me with contempt. May the Lord judge between you and me!"*
>
> —Genesis 16:5

Abraham plays it smart this time and decides to relent, which doesn't bode well for poor Hagar.

> *But Abram said to Sarai, "Behold, your servant is in your power; do to her as you please." Then Sarai dealt harshly with her, and she [Hagar] fled from her [Sarai].*
> —Genesis 16:6

Thus Hagar, a young pregnant girl, sets out alone on a long journey across a foreign land with no provisions, no plan, and very few choices. She is in one of the most vulnerable positions she could possibly imagine. And then, God speaks—and everything changes.

> *The angel of the Lord found her by a spring of water in the wilderness, the spring on the way to Shur. And he said, "Hagar, servant of Sarai, where have you come from and where are you going?" She said, "I am fleeing from my mistress Sarai." The angel of the Lord said to her, "Return to your mistress and submit to her." The angel of the Lord also said to her, "I will surely multiply your offspring so that they cannot be numbered for multitude." And the angel of the Lord said to her, "Behold, you are pregnant and shall bear a son. You shall call his name Ishmael, because the Lord has listened to your affliction....So she called the name of the Lord who spoke to her, "You are a God of seeing," for she said, "Truly here I have seen him who looks after me."*
> —Genesis 16:7–11, 13

In one of my favorite passages in all of scripture, God steps into this broken woman's reality, looks her straight in the eye, and speaks directly to her. He doesn't speak to her about situations in general, but *directly* to the messy and busted up place where she currently resides. He gives no shallow platitudes or quick-fix solutions. God sends His word to intervene in Hagar's life, and it absolutely undoes her.

Hagar quickly realizes that one of the most amazing things about this God who speaks is that when He does, His word always comes from a place of seeing, of hearing, and of knowing. He saw her need. He heard her cry. He knew absolutely everything there was to know about it all. And *then* He spoke.

With that assurance, Hagar continues on. She turns around just like God directed her. She walked right back into a broken-down situation, knowing now that God was with her in the midst of it.

I don't often identify with the heroes of scripture—the bold warriors, the wise judges, the grand kings. I don't see much of myself in any of those types. When God speaks to them in the Bible, I can often justify why He might want to do that. But when God steps in and talks to a woman like Hagar—ousted, unwanted, unnoticed, shamed—I can actually feel something shift in my heart, a hope rising up, a faith growing bold. A burgeoning desire to come near and listen to God's word for myself.

The truth is, God wasn't just speaking to Hagar that afternoon in the wilderness. He wasn't just speaking to Adam and Eve that morning in the garden. He wasn't just speaking to Samuel that night at the temple. In all His words to them, He was speaking to you and to me.

### God's Word Spoken, *to Us*
Has this truth somehow escaped us? Hebrews 4:12 explains "the word of God is living and active." It does more than just exist on a page and tell of a time gone by. God presently reaches into each of our lives as we read and study

scripture. Perhaps one of the reasons we have so readily turned away from our individual study of the Bible is that we don't really believe this. We wrongly view the Bible as some ancient text that we need someone to interpret for us instead of rightly understanding it as God's word being spoken to us—right now, relaying not just information but His very spirit.

I remember how specifically God spoke to me early one morning after a particularly difficult day of mothering. The boys had been absolutely horrid the day before (fighting, fussing, and throwing fits from sunup to sundown), and I had blundered spectacularly in my attempts to mother them.

Frustrated and weary, I had blamed them for more than their ages had the capacity to bear. I had yelled, hollered, and thrown a few fits of my own. That entire night, as they slept peacefully, the sick feeling in the pit of my stomach grew and grew. I had completely failed them that day, been harsher than I needed to be. God had entrusted their tender, young hearts into my hands, and I had mishandled them so. I awoke that morning to find the following verse in my morning reading:

> *The steadfast love of the Lord never ceases; his mercies never come to an end; they are new every morning; great is your faithfulness.*
>
> —Lamentations 3:22–23

God spoke those words directly to me. Ministered right to my muddled mommy-heart as clear as day.

I remember His word confronting me in the midst of an interpersonal mess in which I had become entangled. I had been hurt by people I cared for, felt completely wronged, and become increasingly indignant as a result. And then, right in the middle of teaching a study on the Lord's Prayer one morning, God made it clear that this was no longer an issue of what wrong *they* may have done to *me*, but an issue of what *I* couldn't do for *them*.

I couldn't forgive them. His words practically stung as they tumbled out of my mouth that day "Forgiving one another, as God in Christ forgave you" (Eph. 4:32). More than just an ancient decree or a wise suggestion, those words were a direct command from God to me at that very moment.

I remember furiously scrubbing our kitchen floor during a particularly rough season of life. I had been wrestling for weeks with phantoms from my past. Old hurts, regrets, and unrelenting guilt had taken up residence in my soul. I had been carrying around this perpetual feeling of heart-sickness that I couldn't get out from under. Mid-scrub, the pastor on the radio began teaching on John 4, and God's word to me rang clear.

I set aside the housework and opened my Bible so I could see His words for myself. As I read the familiar story of Jesus and the Samaritan woman, I wept uncontrollably. God reached through the pages of John 4 that day and grabbed me tightly. I realized that day that His word really does speak to us right where we are. It actually intersects our day-to-day lives.

God so deeply wants us to know that He speaks, that He describes Jesus—the most important player in the entire Bible—quite simply as "the word."

> *In the beginning was the Word, and the Word was with God, and the Word was God....And the Word became flesh and dwelt among us.*
>
> —John 1:1, 14

Jesus Christ, the very Word of God wrapped up in flesh and bone. God sent His Word to us, and then the Word Himself began to speak:

> *Seeing the crowds, he went up on the mountain, and when he sat down, his disciples came to him. And he opened his mouth and taught them.*
>
> —Matthew 5:1–2

Indeed, the Word spoke. But I contend that we have distanced ourselves from the Bible, not because of an inability to believe God *has* spoken, but because we lack the present-day assurance that God continues to speak.

Maybe you can somehow wrap your head around the fact that God actually spoke in the past to these historic, big-name biblical players, but perhaps you're much less confident in the fact that God actually speaks to you, right now. In this way, our over-reliance on Bible study materials points not just to a lack of confidence in our ability to understand the Bible on our own, but much more significantly to a lack of confidence in the God who speaks to us through it.

This, more than anything else, threatens to take the life out of our individual Bible study. The very first assurance we must carry with us into any endeavor to study the Bible is that God's word speaks. More pointedly, we must know that God speaks to us through His word, right now.

### God's Word Spoken to Us, *Right Now*

2 Timothy 3:16 gives us great insight into this truth. It tells us that "All Scripture *is breathed out by God.*" The imagery of God breathing out scripture recalls the creation account in the Garden of Eden. Just as God breathed into Adam's nostrils the breath of life, making him a living creature

(Gen. 2:7), He breathes out, He exhales, He *speaks* His word to us through scripture, producing within us new life as well.

The Bible is God's word spoken to us *right now.* This is stated both implicitly and explicitly time and again throughout the entirety of scripture. His word is the means through which God creates within us and accomplishes around us all that He has intended for us. Just as surely as the Lord stepped into Hagar's broken-down mess of a life, looked her straight in the eye, and spoke, He steps into our lives as well.

God has always been and continues to be full of words for His people. A serious, intentional, and continuing commitment to study the Bible is one of the surest ways to hear God. Undoubtedly, one of the greatest challenges we face in hearing God speak is, quite simply, learning to listen. We'll tackle that next.

> *Speak. I'm your servant, ready to listen.*
> —1 Samuel 3:10 MSG

## Chapter 2: Dig in Deeper
Questions for Study and Reflection

1. Scripture teaches that God's word has the power to accomplish. Look up these verses and list what each of them reveals about the abilities and characteristics of God's word.

   ❧ Psalm 107:20

   ❧ John 15:3

   ❧ Acts 20:32

   ❧ 2 Timothy 3:16-17

   ❧ Hebrews 4:12

   ❧ 1 Peter 1:23

   > Which of these abilities or characteristics of God's word brings you the most comfort? Which brings you the most conviction? Be specific. Why?

2. One of the assurances we have from God is that when He speaks, He is always coming from a place of hearing, of seeing, and of knowing. Look up the following verses that illustrate these truths.

   ❧ Genesis 16:1-13

   ❧ Psalm 34:17

   ❧ Jeremiah 20:12

   ❧ John 2:24-25

   ❧ Acts 15:8

   > How does the fact that God hears, sees, and knows before He speaks influence the way you perceive His word?

## Chapter 3: Are You Listening?

*Incline your ear, and come to me; hear, that your soul may live.*

*—Isaiah 55:3*

I remember well the early days of being a brand-new mother. I recall bringing that tiny, six-pound little boy home, placing him in his perfectly-Pottery-Barn-outfitted crib, and then having absolutely no idea what I was supposed to do with him.

We had bought absolutely everything everyone had told us we needed: all the sensory toys, the play mats, the complete *Your Baby Can Read* bundle (I'm dead serious), the crib mirror, and the car seat toys. We had it *all*, only to discover that this precious, tiny, newborn baby did absolutely nothing with any of that stuff. Lesson learned. We didn't buy anything for our next two except more diapers and wipes, which every seasoned mother knows is the real stuff of parenting.

While I may have completely botched a million things along my journey of motherhood (not one of my children ever learned to read as an infant), one thing I know I do consistently well is this: my ear is finely tuned to hear their little voices. I'm so deft at discerning their late-night cries, muffled pleas for help, padded footsteps, and secret conspiracies, that Jacob, my six-year-old, calls it a ninja skill. One mark of a mother is her instinct to listen for her child's voice. When you listen for someone, you assume the reality of his presence and the nearness of his proximity.

In the same way that I have trained my ear to hear my children's voices, we must train our ears to hear God's voice, thus assuming the reality of His presence and the nearness of His proximity.

We do this, first and foremost, by reading our Bibles.

Although God can speak to us through other means (including our beloved Bible studies), He speaks to us most surely through the inspired words of scripture. If you hear nothing else from this book, hear this: *We have no clearer voice from God than the Bible.* As John Piper puts it, "outside the Bible we have fallible, uncertain impressions and messages. Inside the Bible we have rock solid dependable messages."[1]

We must listen to God's voice through the examination of scripture.

Undoubtedly, one characteristic that has always marked the people of God is that they are a people who *listen* to God. Even more than that, they seek out, run to, and pursue an understanding of His word. This is not to say that they have every verse of the Bible memorized, have clear-cut answers to every theological question, or never struggle with questions or doubt. To the contrary, I probably have more questions now than I did when I first began seriously studying the Bible many years ago.

However, Jesus refused to parse words when He defined the essence of discipleship in John 8:31: "If you abide in my word, you are truly my disciples."

---

1. John Piper, "Does God Verbally Speak to Me? *Desiring God,* accessed February 17, 2018, www.desiringgod.org/interviews/does-god-verbally-speak-to-me.

Without exception, following Jesus requires that we dwell near, stick close to, and hold firmly to God's word. I can't read the red-letter words of John 8:31 without being deeply convicted that my attempt to circumvent reading the Bible through any means of Bible study other than *my eyes* on *His word* is a flat-out cop-out. Our individual study of God's word is vitally important when it comes to hearing God speak. We cannot learn to recognize His voice by hearing other people describe it. Listening to God is necessarily experiential. It is something we must do for ourselves.

Given Jesus's description of true discipleship in John 8:31, it shouldn't surprise us that one of the clearly traceable predecessors of the people of God falling away from God is their failure to listen to God.

Like Jesus, the prophets of the Old Testament refused to tread lightly around this topic. The prophet Jeremiah lamented over the people of God's inattention to God's word:

> *I have spoken persistently to you, but you have not listened. You have neither listened nor inclined your ears to hear, although the Lord persistently sent to you all his servants the prophets.*
>
> —Jeremiah 25:3–4

Don't gloss over the repetition of the word *persistent* in those verses. God's voice is a persistent one. As we explored in chapter 2, a deep-rooted belief that God is actually speaking to us right now necessarily precedes a heart-level commitment to lean in close and listen. If a commitment to the process of directly listening to God speak to us through His word is absent, then we are left in need of an intermediary between us and the Bible (for many of us, the Bible study has occupied this place), and that is one of the issues this book purposes to address. When all is said and done, we want to learn to listen to God for ourselves through our personal study of scripture.

## The Struggle Is Real

Listening is a surprisingly difficult exercise, even in our most frequent face-to-face encounters. Many of the same issues that interfere with effective listening in our daily interpersonal endeavors likewise interfere with our ability to hear God speak through scripture. We're going to spend part of this chapter exploring information that can rightly be applied to both types of communication, person-to-person as well as God-to-person, so we can then better home in on some things that apply specifically to our ability to listen to God through scripture.

One of the reasons listening is such a difficult skill to improve is because we take our ability to listen for granted. Instead of rightly understanding listening as a skill we must practice to perfect, we see it as something we are innately wired to do.

And while physiologically this may be true for the majority of us, we must understand that just because we have physically *heard* a message (with our ears) does not mean we have actually *listened* to that message (with our brains). We often wrongly assume that if a message doesn't register in our brain, the other person must not have said it.

On several occasions, Jesus concluded His teaching by saying, "He who has ears to hear, let him hear" (Mark 4:9, 23, Luke 8:8, 14:35). I think it's safe to assume that those who sat in Jesus's audience those days had ears. Jesus knew full well that even if thousands of people had heard Him speaking—physically heard the sound of His voice going out over the crowd—not nearly that many had actually *listened*, opened their hearts to receive His word, considering, weighing, and then moving in accordance to what He had said.

In the same way, are we allowing God's word to merely pass by our ears? Are we neglecting the hard work it takes to consider, weigh, and then move in accordance to what He has said? Are we using an intermediary to relay His message instead of taking the time to hear it for ourselves? And in so doing, are we really listening to God?

## Learning to Listen

Assuming that's the place we all want to be—able to hear God speak to us through His word—how do we get there?

Listening is a complex process that involves selecting, attending to, constructing meaning from, and even remembering a message. It is a required ingredient in the formation and maintenance of every human relationship you have—with your friends, your family members, your coworkers—and it is equally required in the formation and maintenance of your relationship with God.

When God created us as relational beings, He opened up communication between Himself and us as a mutual endeavor. Exodus 33:11 illustrates this: "the Lord used to speak to Moses face to face, as a man speaks to his friend." God intends for a conversation to occur between us and Him, just as when you talk to anybody else in your life. He talks to us, and we listen to Him. We talk to Him, and He listens to us. This is how a relationship with God works.

Good communication between you and your spouse (or friend, or sister) is simply a mirror of what God purposed good communication to look like between you and Him. Like anything else in life worthy of our pursuit, listening to hear God speak through His word requires time, intentionality, and purpose.

The first thing we're going to do as we seek to become better listeners in our individual study of the Bible is identify those things that keep us from listening to God's word effectively.

**Recognizing Your Barriers**

A listening barrier is anything that gets in the way of clear communication, thus hindering your ability to understand what is being said. The barriers that are generally the easiest to recognize are those that are environmental in nature. These are called external barriers to listening, many of which come down to matters of practicality—are you, for example, physically able to hear and focus on what God is saying?

There are also internal barriers to listening that come not from the environment *outside* of you but from the environment *inside* of you. These are things like your thoughts, attitudes, and preconceived notions.

Picture the listening process as something like this:

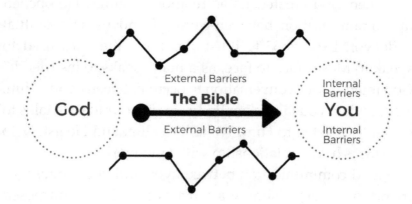

To succeed in listening to God speak through His word, we have to tame both the external and internal barriers that hinder our ability to do so.

## All that noise in your house

I am the mother of three young boys, ages eight, six, and four. Over the course of my tenure as a mother, I have learned that there is no way I am going to have the capacity to listen if any of my children are anywhere in my vicinity. Their need for Cheerios, tape, water, string, the wi-fi password, Pirate's Booty, and lizard bait (all actual requests) trumps my ability to lean in closely and listen to God.

The only time I have been able to consistently carve out for Bible study these past eight years has been in the early mornings before my kids wake up. That works for me because I am naturally more productive in the morning and utterly useless past 9:00 p.m.. But please understand, it does not just happen. My eyes do not magically pop open at 5:15 a.m., nor does the Holy Spirit gently woo me out of my warm bed to come spend a few minutes with my Bible. My alarm rings. I think to myself, "Noooooooooooo," and then I stagger out of my bedroom, down the stairs, and into the kitchen for some coffee. Next, I actually have to open my Bible and begin to read. While this may sound simple, I assure you it is not. Between my Pinterest page, Yahoo News, and Facebook, I have about 60 zillion ways I can spend my early mornings that are in no way related to Bible reading.

Partly because of how difficult it is to clear away all these external barriers so I can listen to God's voice through scripture, I have so often settled for a short devotional. These often consist of no more than a verse or two from the Bible with a paragraph explaining how those verses are applicable. This shortcut solution to my inability to home in on God's word became a habit. What was easiest for me became more important than what was best for me.

While your external distractions and barriers to hearing

God speak through His word may look different from mine, each of us has these barriers and each of us will have to find a way around them. Listening to God through the Bible takes time and effort, and we will always have to sacrifice something else in order to make it happen. What's best for you is rarely what is easiest for you.

## All that noise in your heart and head

Although external barriers can definitely make it a challenge to get into God's word, they are never the root issue. If you're not studying the Bible, it is not because you are a hapless victim of your schedule and commitments; it is because you have made the choice to *not* study the Bible.

One of the more difficult lessons I've learned as I've gone in and out of seasons of intentional time in God's word is that no matter the laundry list of excuses I have for not studying the Bible (which quite often actually includes the laundry), my lack of study always boils down to one of two things: (1) pride or (2) self-absorption. Both of them fall into the category of internal barriers.

It took me forever to recognize these attitudes as barriers, because in no way did I see myself as a prideful, self-absorbed person. To the contrary, those seasons when I fell off the Bible study wagon most often occurred during periods of my life when I was more other-focused than I had ever been before—as a wife and mother of young children. I mean how prideful can you be when a majority of your time is spent picking boogers out of other people's noses, wiping other people's bottoms, and picking dried bits of baby food out of your hair?

Yet still, how many times have I viewed the time needed to study God's word as a disruption to my schedule or somehow less important than the many other tasks I had to complete on any given day? How many days did I neglect God's word, implicitly believing that I could achieve what I needed to achieve without His help or guidance?

No matter how I slice it, lack of dependence on God always boils down to a prideful, self-absorbed heart. Sometimes that pride gets dressed up in a pair of nice-looking heels with a designer business suit to match, and sometimes it's dressed in a milk-stained T-shirt that matches the dried baby food in your hair. Either way, it explicitly or implicitly states, *This is about me, and I got it! I can do this on my own!*

> *In his pride the wicked man does not seek him; in all his thoughts there is no room for God.*
>
> —Psalm 10:4 NIV

## Remembering Not to Forget

I have noticed a fairly consistent pattern when it comes to slipping into these periods of pride and self-absorption that distract me from God's word. Recognizing this has helped me guard against falling into the same old ruts again and again. My observation is this: it is not during the seasons of hardship and struggle that I most intentionally have to set my eyes on God's word, but it is during those seasons of ease and abundance that I am most prone to forget the reality of my daily need for Him.

The Bible warns us of this very thing. Before the Israelites crossed over into the Promised Land, Moses cautioned them of the human propensity to forget God during seasons of abundance:

> *When you have eaten and are satisfied, praise the Lord your God for the good land he has given you. Be careful that you do not forget the Lord your God, failing to observe his commands, his laws and his decrees that*

*I am giving you this day. Otherwise, when you eat and are satisfied, when you build fine houses and settle down, and when your herds and flocks grow large and your silver and gold increase and all you have is multiplied, then your heart will become proud and you will forget the Lord your God, who brought you out of Egypt, out of the land of slavery.*

—Deuteronomy 8:10–14 NIV

Failure to abide in God's word, to lean in and listen to what He has to say, is a red, flashing sign that we are actively forgetting the Lord our God. Interestingly, it was this very forgetfulness that first led to humans falling away from God.

Take a look at this text from Genesis 3, just after Eve so hastily consumed the fruit that the Lord had commanded her not to eat:

*Then the Lord God said to the woman, "What is this that you have done?" The woman said, "The serpent deceived me, and I ate."*

—Genesis 3:13

Depending on the translation you use, that last sentence reads in several different ways:

"The serpent *deceived* me, and I ate" (ESV, NIV).
"The serpent *beguiled* me, and I did eat" (KJV).
"The serpent *tricked* me, and I ate" (NET).

Deceived, tricked, beguiled—all those words convey a clear image of the manner in which Satan enticed Eve away from God. But the literal translation of that word is even more profound. It reads, "The serpent *caused me to forget, and I ate.*"

But what exactly did Satan cause Eve to forget? The

answer is one chapter back in Genesis 2 when God fore-warned:

> *You may surely eat of every tree of the garden, but of the tree of the knowledge of good and evil you shall not eat, for in the day that you eat of it you shall surely die.*
> —Genesis 2:16–17

Eve forgot God and His all-sufficient word to her. As a result, she stepped outside the boundaries of His all-sufficient plan for her. Eve's forgetfulness set a precedent for the rest of humankind. Since the fall of man and woman in Genesis 3, the natural inclination of the human heart has been to forget God's word, so you and I must be vigilant in our efforts to remember.

> *Only take care, and keep your soul diligently, lest you forget the things that your eyes have seen, and lest they depart from your heart all the days of your life.*
> —Deuteronomy 4:9

Undoubtedly, we will face challenges as we listen to hear God speak to us through His word. Understanding these challenges will help us recognize them as they become problematic and then combat them as they begin interfering with our attempts to listen. That alone will go a long way toward making us better listeners.

We can also learn to listen to God for ourselves more effectively by incorporating good listening practices into our Bible study routine.

## Good Listening Practices

Good listening practices are those things you can actively *do* in order to hear more clearly and listen more effectively. In a face-to-face conversation with your best friend, you would seek to maintain eye contact, look for nonverbal cues to aid in understanding, and ask for clarity when needed. All these actions would result in a better understanding of the message she gave. When we read the Bible, we likewise want to be active in our efforts to hear more clearly and listen more effectively.

Here are some important listening practices we want to put into place when God is the one to whom we are listening.

## Posture of Humility

The one thing that opens our ears to hear God's word more than anything else is a posture of humility. We humble ourselves in submission under the authority of God's word as we read, not lord ourselves over it. When you set out to study the scriptures, you must bear in mind that no matter where you sit as you study, you are on holy ground. These are not merely the opinions of people, but the truth of God you are considering. This should deeply impact the manner in which you consider it.

When our primary means of studying scripture is through an intermediary (such as a Bible study book, pastor, or teacher), it becomes easy to justify any problems we might have with the Bible as the fault of the person teaching it.

*He didn't explain it that well.*

*I didn't like her tone.*

*I didn't agree with what she said.*

Those very words have escaped my own mouth on several occasions. Maybe the teacher taught the biblical topic correctly, and maybe he or she did not. Either way, when we use these books, pastors, and teachers as buffers between ourselves and the Bible, we can more easily rationalize distancing ourselves from the text because it at least seems to be coming from a source other than God. But when you are the one reading, thinking about, and seeking the scriptures directly, it becomes very clear where any problem you might have with the text really resides—with God Himself. And this is a critical issue we each have to confront at one point or another.

By all means, we are thoughtful, inquisitive, and teachable as we read through the scriptures, and there is most certainly a correct way to ask questions and wrestle with understanding. However, through all of this, we must not be arrogant, presumptuous, critical, or even casual in the way we approach His word.

God makes no apologies for the fact that there are certain things we simply will not understand, certain questions His word does not answer. In fact, He is quite blunt when He broaches the issue. He says:

> *For my thoughts are not your thoughts, neither are your ways my ways....For as the heavens are higher than the earth, so are my ways higher than your ways and my thoughts than your thoughts.*
>
> —Isaiah 55:8–9

We should not enter into our study of the Bible expecting that we will find every answer to every question. God is in no way required to answer to us. This topic is iterated throughout the biblical narrative. The book of Job does a particularly good job of illustrating it for us.

After losing everything God had ever given him, Job asks the Lord why He had allowed him to suffer such great misery and loss. Job inquires of God:

> *Oh, that I had someone to hear me! I sign now my defense—let the Almighty answer me; let my accuser put his indictment in writing.*
>
> —Job 31:35 NIV

In essence, Job is asking the creator to answer to the created. He is asking the judge to justify Himself. When the Lord replies, instead of answering Job's question, He reminds Job of his limited understanding and perspective as a created being. God asks Job:

> Where were you when I laid the foundation of the earth?
>
> —Job 38:4

> Have you commanded the morning since your days began?
>
> —Job 38:12

> Will you even put me in the wrong? Will you condemn me that you may be in the right? Have you an arm like God?
>
> —Job 40:8–9

For four chapters, the Lord goes on like this. His ultimate point is that He is God; Job is a man. He is sovereign; Job is dependent. He is infinite; Job is finite. He is omniscient; Job is limited. (You and I have a lot in common with Job.)

As uncomfortable as it might make us feel, we don't get to know everything. But we do get to know everything we need. 2 Peter 1:3 assures us of this. Peter tells us that God "has granted to us all things that pertain to life and godliness." And guess what? That area of discomfort that exists between what God *has* made known about Himself, and what He *hasn't* made known about Himself provides us with the perfect soil for our faith to flourish.

> He leads the humble in what is right, and teaches the humble his way.
>
> —Psalm 25:9

## Perspective of Faith

Another good listening practice to incorporate into your study of the Bible is to approach God's word with a perspective of faith.

Hebrews 11:6 reminds us that "without faith it is impossible to please him, for whoever would draw near to God must believe that he exists and that he rewards those who seek him." When we enter into the study of God's word, our default position should be one of trust, that no matter how the text strikes us, presses in on us, or rubs against us, God's word is for our good and sufficient to meet our needs.

First, we must trust that God's word is for our good.

> And now, Israel, what does the Lord your God require of you, but to fear the Lord your God, to walk in all his ways, to love him, to serve the Lord your God with all your heart and with all your soul, and to keep the commandments and statutes of the Lord, which I am commanding you today for your good?
>
> —Deuteronomy 10:12–13

The whole of God's counsel is for our good. This will be a much easier perspective to have as you read through the book of Ephesians rather than, say, the book of Hosea. But either it is *always* true of His word or it is *never* true of His word. If we only sometimes trust Him and what He has communicated to us through His word, choosing which bits and pieces fit neatly into our worldview and discarding those that don't, then we don't really trust Him.

Please hear this: there are portions of the Bible that I have struggled over mightily—the Canaanites being devoted to destruction, the devastation of Sodom and Gomorrah, John the Baptist's beheading, the flood, the fall—on and on. I could point to instances in the Bible where I have thought, *Why,*

*God? How could you allow this?* or *Why would you command this?* or *Couldn't you have stopped this?*

Having faith doesn't mean that we can't wrestle with such questions. However, in our wrestling, we must be faithful in acknowledging that He is God; we are human. And then we must trust Him to be the just, merciful, righteous, and good God that His word tells us He is. From that foundation of trust—in His character, in His intentions, in the integrity of His word—we can work to build our understanding of the text upon solid ground.

As we lean in to listen to God's word with a perspective of faith, we must also trust it to be sufficient to meet our needs. We enter into a study of God's word assuming that through His word, God is ready and able to give us exactly what it is that we need.

In comparing His word to our daily bread (Deut. 8:3), God powerfully conveys the image of His word as giving us the sustenance we need for daily survival. Bible study is not just something we do to gather nice words and ethereal promises; it is the place we go to gain access to those things we need for our day-to-day living—guidance, direction, nourishment, sustenance.

When we come to His word, we come understanding that it contains more wisdom, help, and healing within it than any other source of assistance we might turn to, whether a spouse, a trusted friend, or a favorite Christian writer, speaker, or pastor. That doesn't mean that God can't or won't use these other means to speak to us, but we will find that the best word from someone else will always point us back to His word. We should train ourselves to more regularly begin there, depending less on an intermediary and more on God.

In the book of Second Timothy, the apostle Paul writes as he awaits execution. He warns Timothy of all the hardship and persecution he will most certainly face as he continues to follow Christ. Yet in the midst of all of these warnings, Paul's best piece of advice for Timothy is for him to hold tightly to the scriptures. Paul exhorts:

> *All scripture is given by inspiration of God, and is profitable for doctrine, for reproof, for correction, for instruction in righteousness: that the man of God may be perfect, thoroughly furnished unto all good works.*
> —2 Timothy 3:16–17 KJV

Paul knew that God's word alone could thoroughly equip Timothy for "all good works" that lay before him, including imprisonment and death by stoning. The apostles clung to the scriptures understanding that their very lives depended on them while we allow the very same words to fall to the wayside, insistent that we need something more than, other than, or in addition to God's word to us. The lives and deaths of the early apostles and so many who have gone since prove that God's word is sufficient to meet the needs of our most dire circumstances, and it is equally sufficient to meet our needs as we go about the mundane business of everyday life.

Trust that His word will meet you exactly where you are, whether that is underneath a never-ending pile of laundry, lunches, and milk-stained T-shirts, after the loss of yet another child, or during chemo treatments for the second time this year. I've known women who have endured each of these things, and they all equally amaze me. When we approach the scriptures with this perspective of faith—that it can meet every need we have—we are giving ourselves the ability to listen.

## Patience and Persistence

It takes a long time to become a good listener. Perhaps the

most valuable good listening practice of all comes down to a matter of practicality. You must be willing to patiently persist, to continue daily in your earnest search of God's voice despite your present inability to discern it.

It took many years of consistent and persistent Bible study for me to become confident in my ability to hear God speak through His word. And yet even now, it seems like He goes silent from time to time. There are days (weeks, months) when I read and study scripture only to come away feeling like He's not speaking to me at all. During those times, I remind myself that when someone shouts, I can hear from quite a distance away, but when someone's voice diminishes to a whisper, I must step closer to hear. When I can't hear God, I simply need to come closer. Perhaps He has dropped His voice to a whisper so I will do just that.

When all is said and done, remember this: listening is a discipline and a skill. It will take time to learn how to listen to God's word speak. As in all matters of faith, we must allow ourselves the time needed to grow in this area. If you struggle in your belief of the timeliness, relevance, and proximity of God's word, and thus your propensity to lean in close and listen for yourself, understand that we all do. Lean in anyway. Humble yourself before Him. Be patient. Keep at it, and trust that the Lord will meet you in your efforts.

> *As for that in the good soil, they are those who, hearing the word, hold it fast in an honest and good heart, and bear fruit with patience.*
>
> —Luke 8:15

### Some Bold Assurances

We began this chapter by looking at Jesus's assessment of what makes a true disciple: one who dwells near, listens closely, and remains present in His word. Jesus said, "If you abide in my word, you are truly my disciples" (John 8:31).

I'd like to close this chapter by drawing attention to the astonishing promise Jesus ties to the end of that statement: "and you will know the truth, and the truth will set you free" (John 8:32). I've always found that truth to be utterly astounding and so incredibly bold. *Abide in my word. It will make you free.*

Here, Jesus is telling us that when we hold close to His word, we have every right to expect something from Him in return. He spells out for us in no uncertain terms what it is that we should expect—complete and total freedom. Jesus is making an incredible promise that His word has the power and the ability to absolutely set us free—to liberate us, to exempt us from moral and mortal liability, to deliver us, rescue us, and free us from bondage. Jesus proclaims that *this* is the work that God's word came to do. And He intends for us to count on that.

He intends for us to eagerly expect that God's word will do the miraculous work that it came to do. So as we set out to do as Jesus has instructed—to abide in God's holy word—we must understand this. If we enter into a study of God's word with our eyes and hearts set on anything less than complete and total restoration, utter freedom and liberation, we have altogether misplaced our hopes and expectations.

In the next chapter, we're going to look at those hopes and expectations. We'll see how faulty ones will derail our study of God's word and how having the right ones can absolutely unlock the Bible for you.

> *Oh, that today you would listen as he speaks!*
> —Hebrews 3:7 NET

**Chapter 3: Dig in Deeper**
Questions for Study and Reflection

1. Write out the following verses:

   ❧ Psalm 116:1–2

   ❧ Jeremiah 29:12

   ❧ Psalm 18:6

   ❧ Psalm 5:3

2. What assurance do the people of God have in regard to God's ability and inclination to listen to us?

3. Think about the listening barriers we discussed earlier in this chapter.

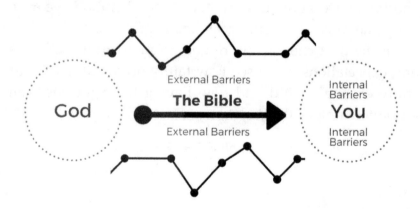

What are your most prominent external barriers to hearing God speak to you through His word? What are your most prominent internal barriers to hearing God speak to you through His word? List some actions or steps you can take to combat each type of barrier. Use the chart below to organize your thoughts.

| My external barriers to hearing God speak | My strategy to combat these barriers |
|---|---|
|  |  |
|  |  |
|  |  |
|  |  |
|  |  |

| My internal barriers to hearing God speak | My strategy to combat these barriers |
|---|---|
|  |  |
|  |  |
|  |  |
|  |  |
|  |  |

## Chapter 4: Hopes and Expectations

*I came that they may have life and have it abundantly.*
—John 10:10

Perhaps the most heartbreaking question someone ever asked God came from the lips of one of the most faithful men to ever live: John the Baptist. Imprisoned, soon to be killed, and riddled with disappointment and doubt, John sent his disciples to ask Jesus this question:

> *Are you the One we've been expecting, or are we still waiting?*
> —Matthew 11:3 MSG

I can only image that John's words cut Jesus straight to the heart. If ever there was a man who should have known that Jesus was the one, the Christ, the Messiah, it was John.

Even before John was born, the angel Gabriel appeared to John's father, telling him that his son's life's work would be to get people ready for Jesus's arrival, to "make ready for the Lord a people prepared" (Luke 1:17). John spent his entire life doing that very thing. Upon seeing Jesus for the first time, John knew so deep down in his bones that Jesus was the one that he cried out, "Behold, the Lamb of God, who takes away the sin of the world!" (John 1:29). John went on to say, "I have seen and have borne witness that this is the Son of God" (John 1:34). If ever there was a man who knew who Jesus was, who had every hope that Jesus would do what He said He was going to do, it was John the Baptist.

But as Jesus began walking out the day-to-day life of His ministry on earth, it looked different than what John might have expected. And John, who had spent his entire life preparing himself and others for Jesus's arrival, found himself in prison for the very work he had been doing on Jesus's behalf.

The Bible doesn't tell us how long John sat in prison, but it was long enough for him to begin questioning his faith in Jesus. Long enough for him to begin second-guessing everything he had seen Jesus do. Long enough for him to begin doubting that Jesus actually was who He said He was. After all, if Jesus was truly the Messiah, what on earth was He doing? Why would Jesus allow John's captivity to continue? At a certain point, John's questions became so deep and urgent that he called some of his disciples to him in prison and sent them to clarify with Jesus once and for all:

> *Are you the One we've been expecting, or are we still waiting?*
>
> —Matthew 11:3 MSG

Needless to say, John's expectations for the Messiah, to whom John had dedicated his entire life, had not been met. As a result, he became blind to the greater work that Jesus was doing. Jesus answered John's disciples:

> *Go back and tell John what's going on: The blind see, The lame walk, Lepers are cleansed, The deaf hear, The dead are raised, The wretched of the earth learn that God is on their side. Is this what you were expecting?*
>
> —Matthew 11:4–6 MSG

Jesus wasn't doing less than John had hoped. He was doing far more. But the difficult circumstances of John's life clouded his view of the bigger picture. Because faulty expectations can blind us to a reality even greater than the one for which we had hoped, we must understand what we can rightly expect from God and His word. We must understand exactly what it is that He promises the Bible will do.

But before we get there, we must identify the things that are blinding us to the greater reality. So let's begin with our own expectations. What have *you* been hoping, or expecting, the Bible to do for you?

Maybe you've never really thought about it this way, but we each carry expectations with us into every situation— even our study of scripture. If you've found your attempts to study the Bible on your own disappointing and unfruitful, then chances are you've got some unmet expectations.

Jesus's assertion in John 8 that His word will make us free sets the bar pretty high for what we can expect from the Bible. His promise is nothing less than complete and total freedom. Yet despite this absolutely remarkable promise, time and again I see fellow Christians discouraged and disappointed in their attempts to study the Bible.

When asked what keeps them from spending more time in God's word, one woman said that she wasn't sure she would get anything out of it. Another one answered, "I'm afraid that what I read and what I hope for won't come to be." These two women voiced concerns that many of us share, that God's word won't meet our expectations—that it will be found lacking, incomplete, or insufficient to do what we hope it will do.

As a result, many of us look to sources outside the Bible in some sort of vain hope that there might be something better—something more sufficient, something more able, something more capable of meeting our needs than God's very word. And this is where it becomes necessary to take a close look at our expectations of God and His word.

Often, there is a gap somewhere between our expectations and hopes of what God's word can do and the actual reality of what God's word does. John Maxwell once said, "Disappointment is the gap that exists between expectation and reality."[2] If you've been disappointed by your attempts to study the Bible, there's a gap of disappointment that probably looks something like this in your mind....

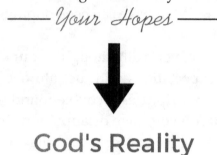

# God's Reality

But my hunch is that the discrepancy between our hopes and God's reality doesn't look like the picture above, but more like the picture below...

# God's Reality

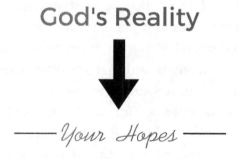

Here's my point: If God's word isn't meeting our expectations, maybe we have the wrong expectations. Let's

---

2. John Maxwell, "5 Reasons Why Dreams Don't Take Flight," accessed February 17, 2018, http://www.johnmaxwell.com/cms/images/uploads/ads/5_Reasons_Why_dreams_Dont_take_Flight.pdf.

take a few minutes to identify what we can expect from God's word so we can then adjust our expectations of His word to line up with His intentions for His word.

**My Expectations for Bible Study**

Take some time to think about what you expect studying God's word will do for you and make some notes in the space below. Be as specific as you can be. I've given you a few prompts to consider.

**I expect that studying the Bible will...**

**In the past, I have felt disappointed in Bible study because...**

**I get discouraged when I try to study the Bible because...**

**I don't study the Bible because...**

Although I can't peer over your shoulder to see what you've written, I can tell you what I discovered when I asked myself these questions. My expectations for Bible study were almost exclusively self-centered. More often than not, my focus as I entered into the study of God's word was *What is this going to do for* me? or *What am I going to get out of this today?* After years of Bible study disappointments, discouragements, and do-overs, I've learned that in making myself the point of Bible study, I was missing much of what the Bible offers.

The Bible is not a self-help book (in fact, it's not really about you at all). We'll discuss this Bible study error in more depth in chapter 6, but for now, let's turn our attention to what the author of the Bible says we can rightly expect from His word.

## What Can We Expect from God's Word?

### We can expect God's word to work.

The Bible claims to be different than any book ever written since the words within the Bible are said to be God's very words written by human hands. God's words are different than our words in that they always carry with them an accomplishing force. When He speaks, whatever He speaks is *always* accomplished. The Lord explains it like this:

*For as the rain and the snow come down from heaven and do not return there but water the earth, making it bring forth and sprout, giving seed to the sower and bread to the eater, so shall my word be that goes out from my mouth; it shall not return to me empty, but it shall accomplish that which I purpose, and shall succeed in the thing for which I sent it.*

—Isaiah 55:10–11

At 7:30 each school night, I walk into our boys' playroom and declare, "Time for bed!" Some nights my boys are eager to please and obey my words quickly. Other nights there is mumbling, grumbling, pleading, protesting, whining, and foot-dragging. Much to my chagrin, my declaration of bedtime lacks the power to actually produce an immediate bedtime. God's word lacks no such power. It succeeds in actually doing something within the one who consumes it. Just as His word produced light, land, and life in Genesis 1, it grows, it produces, and it bears down heavily with grace and truth as it is spoken over us. God's word *effectively affects us.* His word alone has the ability to do this. Whether or not we have the ability to perceive God's word working within us does not change the reality that it is. God's word works.

## We can expect God's word to engage.

The author of Hebrews describes God's word as *living* and *active:*

*For the word of God is living and active, sharper than any two-edged sword, piercing to the division of soul and of spirit, of joints and of marrow, and discerning the thoughts and intentions of the heart.*

—Hebrews 4:12

I want you to slow down and think about the implications of such a claim. Being alive and active, God's word has the ability to *read us* as we read it. It sees all that is within us and then proceeds to sift the good from the bad, the wheat from the chaff. It does not sit paralyzed on a shelf, decrepit and stale, as if burdened by the weight of its own existence. It is a living and breathing revelation *of* God, *from* God with which we're meant to engage. We must read it ourselves, take hold of it ourselves, wrestle with it ourselves, and submit our own lives to it. We don't want a passive understanding of God's word that comes from someone else shrinking it down or sizing it up, but a deep and abiding knowledge of His word that can only be attained by actively grappling with it ourselves. To do this, we must personally engage with our Bibles and enter into our study of His word expecting that it will engage us as we engage it.

## We can expect God's word to give faith.

One of the self-proclaimed abilities of scripture is to produce faith within those who hear it. Romans 10:17 tells us, "So faith comes from hearing, and hearing through the word of Christ." In short, there is no faith without knowledge of the gospel. God's word purposes to produce and strengthen belief within those of us who seek Him. This purpose is explicitly proclaimed many times in scripture:

> [B]ut these are written so that you may believe that Jesus is the Christ, the Son of God, and that by believing you may have life in his name.
> —John 20:31

> Truly, truly, I say to you, whoever hears my word and believes him who sent me has eternal life. He does not come into judgment, but has passed from death to life.
> —John 5:24

*I write these things to you who believe in the name of the Son of God, that you may know that you have eternal life.*

—1 John 5:13

God produces and grows the faith of His people through His word. No matter how encouraging, uplifting, beneficial, or eloquent the words of a Christian writer, teacher, or speaker may be, only God's words have this kind of faith-producing power. The very best we who teach, write, or speak *about* God's word can hope to do is point people deeper *into* God's word. His word is the genesis of all faith.

## We can expect God's word to fight on our behalf.

Ephesians 6:11–12 admonishes Christians to put on the "armor of God" so they can "be strong," "stand against the schemes of the devil," and "wrestle against...the spiritual forces of evil." Among the defensive weapons God has given us are truth, righteousness, peace, faith, and salvation. They are described as the belt, the breast plate, the shoes, and the shield, in that order. These things protect us from the enemy's attacks.

The one and only weapon God has given us with which to fight back is His word, which is described as the "sword of the Spirit" (Eph. 6:17). In the spiritual realm, *God's word* is the only thing that has the power to destroy our enemy. We see Jesus illustrating the offensive power of God's word during His temptation in the wilderness as recorded in Matthew 4:1–11 and Luke 4:1–13. Jesus goes toe to toe with the enemy only through the use of God's word, and in both accounts, the devil left him. Likewise, the Lord has given us His word so we might wield it as needed. As James 4:7 instructs, "Resist the devil, and he will flee from you."

Is the enemy attacking your marriage? Fight back. Is the enemy seeking your children? Fight back. Is the enemy accusing you (Rev. 12:10), deceiving you (John 8:44, Rev. 20:7–8), stealing from you (Mark 4:14–15, John 10:10), tempting you (Matt. 4:1–11), looking to destroy you (Rev. 9:11)? Fight back. Fight back by entrenching yourself in God's word so you can skillfully wield the truth when attacked by the enemy's lies. God's word fights for us.

## We can expect God's word to give wisdom.

In the years I've spent teaching Bible studies, women have told me time and again how difficult it is to read the Bible, how discouraging it is not to understand it, and how incapable and unable they feel when it comes to working through it on their own. This helps explain why we so often turn to pastors, teachers, and other Bible study resources to guide us through our study of the Bible. As I shared in the introduction to this book, I've been there. I really do understand. But God's word has an answer to that:

> If any of you lacks wisdom, let him ask God, who gives generously to all without reproach, and it will be given him.
>
> —James 1:5

> [T]hat the God of our Lord Jesus Christ, the Father of glory, may give you the Spirit of wisdom and of revelation in the knowledge of him.
>
> —Ephesians 1:17

God provides us with the wisdom we need to understand His word. Bible studies, devotionals, and commentaries often offer us a fast-track method for understanding the Bible, which is admittedly appealing and can be, at times or for certain seasons, very beneficial. But I suggest that perhaps wisdom—which the Bible urges us to pursue (Prov. 3:13, 4:5–8)—goes deeper than a mere understanding.

What if wisdom comes when we linger for a bit in those places we can't immediately understand? When we sit uncomfortably in a text and ask God to reveal to us those things we can't see for ourselves?

In a culture that demands instant gratification, we want so badly for every word of the Bible to be immediately applicable that we forgo the reality that it is a *supernatural* word, whose application is not limited to immediate results in the physical world, but remains unapologetically focused on the deep and lasting restoration of our hearts, minds, and souls. Chances are you're not going to understand every word of the Bible as you read it. It's an intricate text composed of 66 books, each of which are entrenched in a specific historical time, context, and culture, written by more than 40 people in at least eight genres of literature over a period of more than 1,600 years. If that's not the least bit intimidating to you, then some sort of arrogance is certainly at play. However, Psalm 119:130 assures us, "The unfolding of your words gives light; it imparts understanding to the simple." Give God's word the opportunity to do what it says it will do. You can expect that His word will make you wise.

## We can expect God's word to reveal.

Just as Hebrews 4:12 tells us that God's word can judge the thoughts and intentions of the heart, James describes God's word as a mirror that reveals us as we really are.

*But be doers of the word, and not hearers only, deceiving yourselves. For if anyone is a hearer of the word and not a doer, he is like a man who looks intently at his natural face in a mirror. For he looks at himself and goes away and at once forgets what he was like. But the one who looks into the perfect law, the law of liberty, and perseveres, being no hearer who forgets but a doer who acts, he will be blessed in his doing.*

—James 1:22–25

One of the inescapable maladies of the human heart is that it is bent toward self-deception. Certain seasons, times, and circumstances of life may grant us glimpses of our true selves, but absent God's word, we are the one who "goes away and at once forgets what he looks like." When we devote ourselves to a study of God's word, it is paramount to taking a long look in the mirror, intentionally seeking out the imperfections, false beliefs, and accepted lies that mar our hearts. Indeed, as the prophet Jeremiah laments in Jeremiah 17:9, "The heart is deceitful above all things, and desperately sick; who can understand it?" Only the one who created us and redeems us can accurately reveal us.

Even more significant than the ability of God's word to reveal *us* to us is its ability to reveal *God* to us. The Bible is the means through which God most prominently reveals Himself to us. 1 Samuel 3:21 says, "the Lord revealed himself to Samuel at Shiloh by the word of the Lord." In Ephesians 3:4, Paul writes, "When you read this, you can perceive my insight into the mystery of Christ." If you want to know Christ with more certainty, with more intimacy, and with more understanding, meet with Him in and through the words of the Bible. It is the primary means through which He reveals Himself to His people.

## We can expect God's word to give life.

Perhaps the most remarkable characteristic of God's word is its ability to give life to those who love it. Each of us has sinned and fallen short of the glory of God (Rom. 3:23). Each of us is spiritually dead because of sins and trespasses (Col. 2:13). Left to our own devices, each of us has made and will continue to make choices that would ultimately lead to our demise. As Proverbs 14:12 aptly puts it, "There is a way that seems right to a man, but its end is the way to death."

Thankfully, ours is a God "who gives life to the dead" and who "calls into existence the things that do not exist" (Rom. 4:17). Just as God breathed life into the very first man in the Garden of Eden, thus making him a living creature, God uses His holy scriptures, which have been "breathed out by God" (2 Tim. 3:16), to awaken our souls from death to life. Through His word, God makes known to us the path of life (Ps. 16:11). Through it, He instructs us, "This is the way, walk in it" (Isa. 30:21). Indeed, as Psalm 119:93 proclaims, "I will never forget your precepts, for by them you have given me life."

## Examining Our Expectations

When Jesus began His public ministry, many of the very people who had been eagerly awaiting the coming Messiah completely missed His presence among them. They were looking for a Messiah who would come and deliver them from Roman bondage and establish an earthly political kingdom in which they would be the rulers. When Jesus gave Himself up to be arrested, tried, convicted, and crucified, it was clear to them that He could not be the one they were waiting on. He simply didn't live up to their expectations.

What the Jewish people missed, and what we should be careful not to miss now, is that Jesus didn't come to meet our expectations but to exceed them. He did not come to merely free us from physical earthly bondage but from an eternal, spiritual bondage. He did not come to cure the maladies of our bodies but of our souls. He did not come to establish a kingdom for us here on earth but in heaven. Many of our individual Bible study attempts are snuffed out because our expectations of what we believe God's word should do don't line up with what He has designed His word to do. As a result, we walk away from our efforts disappointed, convinced that either we're doing something wrong or that God's word is less than what we had hoped for.

While we humans have the propensity to train our eyes and hearts steadfastly on what *is*, God's perpetual longing for us is that we would put our hope in what *is to come*—that we would turn our attention away from quick fixes and shortcuts and to the harder work of complete and total freedom.

It's time for us to set our eyes on the real work that God's word came to do. It's time for us to loosen our grip on all our hopes for the here and now so we can focus more deliberately on what is yet to come. May we dive into our study of His word with the unabashed belief that it will be even more than all we have hoped.

> *My soul, wait thou only upon God; for my expectation*
> *is from him.*
>
> —Psalm 62:5 KJV

## Chapter 4: Dig in Deeper
Questions for Study and Reflection

1. Can you think of a time when you were disappointed in God? Make note of that instance in the space below.

    I was disappointed in God when...


2. Fill in the chart below regarding the situation you wrote about in #1.

| My hopes for the situation were... | The reality of the situation turned out to be... |
|---|---|
|  |  |

3. Now take some time to filter the situation through the truth of God's word, which tells us that "for those who love God all things work together for good" (Rom. 8:28). Ask God to reveal to you the things He might be or has been working out in you through the situation. How might God be using that situation to point you toward greater hope?


4. How do your expectations of Bible study line up with what God has designed His word to do? Where do your hopes for what God's word should do fall short of what God's word has the ability to do?

# Chapter 5: A Lasting Motivation

*And so the Lord says, "These people say they are mine.*
*They honor me with their lips, but their hearts are far*
*from me. And their worship of me is nothing but man-*
*made rules learned by rote."*
—Isaiah 29:13 NLT

Our middle son was 20 months old the day my husband and I carried him into Texas Children's Hospital for an appointment with a pediatric oncologist. The week before, while hoisting him into a shopping cart at Target, his shirt had pulled up, revealing a lump on his sternum that had inexplicably appeared overnight. Later that day, we saw our pediatrician, who sent us for an X-ray, which led to a sonogram. Days later, Dr. Pate called to tell us that she believed the knot on Jacob's chest was a tumor and that she was transferring us to the care of a pediatric oncologist. The tumor had certain characteristics that made the oncologist "uncomfortable" and prone to believe that it was likely malignant. There would be an MRI, a biopsy, and then surgery to remove the tumor.

The weeks that followed were some of the most difficult weeks our family has yet to endure. Those weeks tested everything my husband and I thought we knew to be true about God.

One of our greatest struggles during that period was knowing how to pray. Should we pray for our son to be healed? Miraculously and instantaneously made well? Should we pray for God's will in the situation, no matter what that may be? And more importantly, what would those prayers reveal about our motivations? Would they reveal that we knew God to be good and true and steadfast no matter the outcome of the test results? Or would they reveal a faith that was fragile and conditional and dependent on the ease of our situation?

Chris and I knew that praying for the right thing with the wrong motivation was no better than praying for the wrong thing. Period. Motivations are behind every single thing we say or do. And our motivations tell the true story of our faith.

If our expectations reveal what we hope for, our motivations reveal why we want those things in the first place. As I've had an increasing number of opportunities to write, teach, and speak publicly over the last few years, some of the most difficult terrain I've traversed has been over the rocky road of my motivations. As my voice has become progressively more public, I have found it increasingly necessary to ask myself *Why?* more often.

- Why are you saying/writing/posting that?
- Why are you saying yes to this opportunity?
- Why are you saying no?
- Why did that comment, remark, or reply bother you so much?
- What's your goal/focus/hope in all of this anyway?

These questions, as difficult as they can be to answer at times, help keep me honest. They serve the important function of testing my motivations. Motivations reveal the *why* behind our actions, and the *why* matters greatly.

Unchecked motivations, perhaps even more than misguided hopes and expectations, can derail even the most fervent attempt to meet God in His word. Have you paused lately to consider why you study the Bible, feel like you *should* study the Bible, or struggle so greatly to maintain your study of the Bible? Our motivations matter when it comes to Bible study, and our motivations will dictate how we go about that study.

## A God Who Questions

Jesus demonstrated the depth of His concern for our motives by engaging this topic on an individual basis during His ministry on earth. It seems that He was constantly addressing the motivations of a person's heart, so much that at times He seemed far less concerned with what someone was doing than why they were doing it.

Take a look at the following dialogues Jesus had with those He encountered.

With the rich young man:

> *And behold, a man came up to him, saying, "Teacher, what good deed must I do to have eternal life?" And he said to him, "Why do you ask me about what is good?"*
> —Matthew 19:16–17

With the disciples of the Pharisees:

> *"Teacher, we know that you are true and teach the way of God truthfully, and you do not care about anyone's opinion, for you are not swayed by appearances. Tell us, then, what you think. Is it lawful to pay taxes to Caesar, or not?" But Jesus, aware of their malice, said, "Why put me to the test, you hypocrites?"*
> —Matthew 22:16–18

With His own disciples:

> *Now when Jesus was at Bethany in the house of Simon the leper, a woman came up to him with an alabaster flask of very expensive ointment, and she poured it on his head as he reclined at table. And when the disciples saw it, they were indignant, saying, "Why this waste? For this could have been sold for a large sum and given to the poor." But Jesus, aware of this, said to them, "Why do you trouble the woman?"*
>
> —Matthew 26:6–10

Jesus asked these questions not for His benefit, but for theirs. God's questions always serve at least one purpose. They provide us with the opportunity to evaluate our own hearts and repent where necessary. His questions are one of the many evidences of His very great mercy toward us.

## Digging for Answers

In questioning us, God is seeking to reveal our motives, to move beyond the possible superficiality of our actions to the bare authenticity of our hearts. It is in this way that He cares not just *that* we study His word, but *why* we study it. And although motivations can be nearly impossible for us to discern in our humanity ("The heart is deceitful above all things, and desperately sick; who can understand it?" Jer. 17:9), God is able to untangle even the most mixed-up motives. We'll address that later in the chapter. But first, what *is* the proper motivation for studying God's word?

> *For Christ's love compels us, because we are convinced that one died for all, and therefore all died. And he died for all, that those who live should no longer live for themselves but for him who died for them and was raised again.*
>
> —2 Corinthians 5:14–15 NIV

Scripture is very clear that the motivating force behind everything we do—that which compels us, constrains us, urges us, and quite literally holds us together and impels us forward—is love for Christ. A deep and abiding love for Christ that originates not from us, not from anything in us that is able to love so purely, but from *His love* for us.

> *We love because he first loved us.*
> —1 John 4:19

If anything other than this love drives us into a study of scripture—whether duty, obligation, guilt, or requirement—then our study will be driven by religiosity and rules, and we will quickly become discouraged or lose interest. I know this not because I've never studied with these motives, but because I have so often studied with these motives.

When I first became a Christian in my 20s, I was completely mystified by God's command to us that we must love Him. I couldn't wrap my head around how you could *command* someone to love you. You can command someone to obey you, to follow you, to do any number of things on your behalf, but you can't simply command someone to love you.

Yet there it is, written in those deep red letters. Jesus commands us to love:

> *"Teacher, which is the great commandment in the Law?"*
> *And he said to him, "You shall love the Lord your God*
> *with all your heart and with all your soul and with all*
> *your mind. This is the great and first commandment."*
> —Matthew 22:36–38

As much as I wanted to admire the sentiment behind this great command, I simply couldn't. Not because I didn't *want* to love God, but because I feared so greatly that I wouldn't be able to do so. How good of a Christian was I going to be if I couldn't even nail down "the great and first" commandment?

When I became a Christian, I didn't have that immediate, overwhelming love for Christ that I heard some people describe. That concerned me greatly because I wanted that feeling, but I simply did not have it. I couldn't have realized it at the time, but my heart had grown so calloused over years of hurts, difficulties, and sin in my life that it had become difficult for me to love *anything* well. I accepted God's word to be true and came to know His salvation before I even possessed the ability to love Him. I remember during that season of my life, shortly after I began following the Lord, the only thing I could really pray for was that God would cause me to love Him. I would confess, "Lord, I know I don't love you like I should, but for the life of me, I cannot will that into existence. So if you want me to love you, you're going to have to make that happen." I didn't know how He would accomplish such a thing in me, but I knew that He could. I clung to this verse as if it were a lifeline:

> And I will give them one heart, and a new spirit I will put within them. I will remove the heart of stone from their flesh and give them a heart of flesh, that they may walk in my statutes and keep my rules and obey them. And they shall be my people, and I will be their God.
>
> —Ezekiel 11:19–20

I focused my attention and efforts on coming to know God and His word. As I read and studied and considered the Bible, He grew in me a love for Him that I never could have imagined I would possess. He did this for me through His word before I even had the ability to understand what I was reading. This is how it works: Love for God motivates us to know His word. Knowing His word creates within us a love for God.

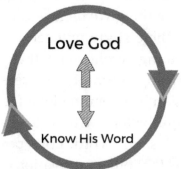

It's a circular relationship in which God's love calls you to action, and that action leads you more deeply into God's love. One catapults you into the next, and the process begins again. Deuteronomy 6 makes clear for us the interrelatedness between loving God and knowing His word.

> *Love the* LORD *your God with all your heart and with all your soul and with all your strength. These commandments that I give you today are to be on your hearts. Impress them on your children. Talk about them when you sit at home and when you walk along the road, when you lie down and when you get up. Tie them as symbols on your hands and bind them on your foreheads. Write them on the door frames of your houses and on your gates.*
>
> —Deuteronomy 6:5–9 NIV

Do you see it there? Verse 5: Love God. Verses 6, 7, 8, and 9: Know His word. The Lord not only tells us what His greatest command is—what He wants for us and from us above all else—but He also graciously reveals to us how to do that: by constantly keeping His word in our sights.

We can't claim love for God if we have no knowledge of His word, and without love for God, we have no lasting motivation to know His word. When motivated by an immediate need to fix a problem or get an answer, we will likely grab the thing we believe can get us there most quickly. Often a Bible study will serve us well, and there is absolutely nothing wrong with that. I reach for Bible studies on specific topics for this very reason. But when our primary motivation is a genuine love for Christ that seeks only to know Him better, we'll go to the place where He most clearly resides: His word. Love possesses a patience and steadfastness that other motivations lack.

## Mixed-Up Motives

My favorite hymn—"Come Thou Fount of Every Blessing" written by Robert Robinson—gives voice to one of the ongoing struggles all who follow Christ must face. It also reminds us of the solution that has already been put into place on our behalf.

> Prone to wander, Lord, I feel it
> Prone to leave the God I love
> Here's my heart, oh, take and seal it
> Seal it for Thy courts above.

If your heart wanders, know that mine does, too. As human beings living in a fallen world, we are constantly prone to wander away from God. Our hearts, our minds, our desires, and our motivations all need constant course-correction to stay bent toward God. So that's what we do; we constantly course-correct.

We *remind ourselves* of our tendency to drift, to pursue God with the wrong motives:

> *And he did what was right in the eyes of the Lord, yet not with a whole heart.*
>
> —2 Chronicles 25:2

We *recognize* that even when we aren't able to discern our mixed-up motives, God remains perfectly able:

> *Jesus answered them, "Truly, truly, I say to you, you are seeking me, not because you saw signs, but because you ate your fill of the loaves.*
>
> —John 6:26

We *request* that God make pure our motives before Him:

> *Create in me a clean heart, O God, and renew a right spirit within me.*
>
> —Psalm 51:10

We *repent* where we fall short:

> *Against you, you only, have I sinned and done what is evil in your sight, so that you may be justified in your words and blameless in your judgment.*
>
> —Psalm 51:4

And finally, we *rely* fully on God's ability to restore us. Believing that His love for us trumps all our weaknesses, stumbles, mistakes, and mixed-up motivations:

> *[F]or whenever our heart condemns us, God is greater than our heart, and he knows everything.*
>
> —1 John 3:20

This constant need for course-correction might seem daunting, but I assure you it doesn't have to be. Perhaps you've spent the last 10 years of your life wandering away from God and His word. Or maybe it's only been the last 10 minutes. Perhaps you've wandered away from God in huge ways, making all the biggest mistakes you could possibly make—failing, faltering, and falling in grand-scale form. Or maybe you've simply slipped up a little, stumbling slightly off course. (God knows I've done my fair share of both.)

I don't know where exactly you are as you read this, but as my friend Teal so wisely reminded me, no matter how far away you are, returning to God always comes down to the exact same process. Stop what you're doing. Turn from the wrong. Turn toward God. If you've messed up in the biggest way possible, stop what you're doing. Turn from the wrong. Turn toward God. If you're just slightly off-kilter, stop what you're doing. Turn from the wrong. Turn toward God. No matter how far away you've wandered, remember the five Rs of course-correction and get back on track.

- *Remind* yourself of your tendency to drift, to pursue God with the wrong motives.

- *Recognize* that even when you aren't able to discern your mixed-up motives, God remains perfectly able.

- *Request* that God make pure your motives before Him.

- *Repent* where you fall short.

- *Rely* fully on God's ability to restore you.

**The Heart of the Matter**

Our motivations matter, but God's grace is so much greater than our failures. I'd be lying if I said I awoke yearning, thirsting, and hungering for God's word each and every morning. Truth be told, some days I simply don't feel like reading my Bible. Some days I don't want to spend my time or invest my energy in the determined study of His word. Sometimes I want nothing more than a shortcut to get me where I want to go. I pray that one day I will reach a level of spiritual maturity where that simply is not the case. Until then, I've developed these rules of thumb to guide me on such occasions. Perhaps you'll find them helpful.

First, I act in obedience. Second, I pray for a willing, pliable, and attentive heart. And finally, when necessary, I go back to the basics.

- ❧ *Act in obedience.* Acting in obedience means spending time in God's word even on those days I don't feel like it. Obedience is foundational to the life of a follower of Christ, not because we're legalists, but because we're devoted to the one we follow. Jesus said, "If you love me, you will keep my commandments" (John 14:15). Sometimes, days are missed, or my reading time is cut short by the early morning awakening of a four-year-old, or by a dishwasher demanding to be unloaded. These things happen. As Sara Wallace explains, "We don't read our Bible to feel better about ourselves or to make God feel better about us. Time in God's Word is a means of experiencing His grace, not earning it."[3] We obey His command to meditate on His word day and night because we believe that knowing Him better is the very best thing for us *even when we don't feel like it.*

- ❧ *Pray.* As I am acting in obedience by reading His word, I pray for a willing, pliable, and attentive heart. I confess my lack of interest and enthusiasm, and I ask God to rightly orient my heart toward His word. I remember God's promise from Ezekiel 11:19–20 and trust in His ability to make good on His promises.

- ❧ *Go back to the basics.* Experiencing hit-or-miss days here and there when you struggle to get into God's word is one thing. A prolonged season of separation from God's word is another. But goodness, I've been there. Life gets

---

3. Sara Wallace, *The Gospel-Centered Mom* (Coeur d'Alene, ID: Minuteman Press, 2014), 48.

heavy, situations get hard, and we all constantly get busted up by this broken world we live in. In the midst of all this, we can so easily draw away from the one thing we need most desperately to draw near to.

When I get caught up in one of these prolonged seasons of separation from God, I find it helpful to go back to the basics—to push aside for a time the weighty theological issues, to skip over the texts that are so very difficult to understand (just for now!), and to decidedly turn my attention to the one thing that will give me some lasting motivation: His very great love for us. This theme is woven throughout the fabric of the entire Bible, but where do you hear it most loudly proclaimed? Go there. Reread that story. Take in that book. Memorize those verses. Lay those words up in your heart. Bind them as a sign on your hand. Keep them as frontlets between your eyes (Deut. 11:18). Do whatever it takes for you to allow His love to rightly motivate you in your study of His word.

Human motivations are fickle and can be layered and layered upon each other. Sometimes I go out of my way to be kind to my husband simply because I love him, and sometimes I do so in the hopes that he'll overlook my recent purchases at Ann Taylor. The latter motivation doesn't necessarily negate the former one, but I mustn't mix up the two.

The Bible acknowledges the complexity of the human heart with all its many motivations and warns us to be wary of the *why* behind our endeavors. In our pursuit of a better understanding of scripture, we must be willing to constantly ask ourselves *why* in order to identify those motivations that come between God's word and us. Once we do so, we can remove those barriers and then turn our attention to God's word itself.

## Chapter 5: Dig in Deeper
Questions for Study and Reflection

Throughout scripture, God uses questions to uncover the motivations of a person's heart and unearth the deep-seated beliefs regarding who He is. Read the following passages that demonstrate God questioning someone in scripture. Imagine that He is asking you that very question. How would you reply?

1. Passage to Read: Matthew 9:27–31
   Question to Consider: "Do you believe that I am able to do this?"
   Your Answer:

2. Passage to Read: Matthew 16:13–20
   Question to Consider: "But who do you say that I am?"
   Your Answer:

3. Passage to Read: Genesis 3:1–9
   Question to Consider: "Where are you?"
   Your Answer:

4. Passage to Read: Mark 8:11–13
   Question to Consider: "Why does this generation seek a sign?"
   Your Answer:

# Part II
# A Simple Solution

In chapters 1 through 5, we did a significant amount of work exploring the Bible study dilemma and unearthing the reasons we are so quick to pick up a Bible study in lieu of the Bible. All this work has been good and necessary, but there remains a glaring possibility regarding our over-reliance on Bible study materials that we have yet to consider. *Maybe we just don't know how to study the Bible on our own.* Maybe that's why we reach for the Bible study.

If that's where you find yourself, I'm here to help. The next two chapters are designed to provide you with the only two things you need to successfully study the Bible on your own: the right perspective and a good process. So now that we've identified the problem, let's start implementing a solution.

# Chapter 6: The Right Perspective

*For this commandment that I command you today is not too hard for you, neither is it far off. It is not in heaven, that you should say, "Who will ascend to heaven for us and bring it to us, that we may hear it and do it?" Neither is it beyond the sea, that you should say, "Who will go over the sea for us and bring it to us, that we may hear it and do it?" But the word is very near you. It is in your mouth and in your heart, so that you can do it.*

—Deuteronomy 30:11–14

The Bible is an intimidating read. I get this. It's big (very big). It's old (very old). Depending on the translation you have, it may even contain words like *ye*, *thee*, *thy*, and *thine*. I don't know about you, but I spent a fair amount of energy in high school avoiding books with those very characteristics. As I shared in the introduction, I used to be so intimidated by the Bible that I read just about everything I could *about* the Bible in order to avoid having to read the actual Bible. I successfully found my way around Bible study for many years. One day it dawned on me that although I knew *about* the Bible, I did not *know the Bible*. I did not know that God could speak directly to me through His written word. I did not know how it would make itself part of me, how it would grow me and pursue me. That it would both wound me and heal me. That it would confront me and reveal me to me and make known to me the depths of His love for me. I could not have known these things because I did not know the Bible.

Maybe you're in that very place right now. The good news is that you don't have to stay there.

No matter how impossible individual Bible study may seem from where you are right now, God is not a God of confusion. To the contrary, He is the God of illumination. He meant for us to read, know, and understand His word because through it He reveals Himself. We march confidently into Bible study with this as our assurance.

> *The unfolding of your words gives light; it imparts understanding to the simple.*
> —Psalm 119:130

It couldn't be much clearer. You don't have to be a brainiac to understand the Bible. Any difficulty we have in comprehending God's word is much more a spiritual matter than an intellectual one. No matter what your level of education, intellectual ability, cultural background, or religious pedigree (or lack thereof), you can understand God's word. He has specifically designed it so.

The first and biggest mistake you can make in regard to studying the Bible is to begin with the assumption that you won't be able to understand it. In assuming you won't be able to understand it, you are merely priming yourself to not understand it. You *can* understand it. But please don't hear me say that you will easily understand it. If Bible study is difficult for you, that's because it's supposed to be difficult. Even the apostle Peter expressed difficulty in understanding the scriptures. In 2 Peter 3:16 he wrote, "There are some things in them [Paul's writings] that are hard to understand, which the ignorant and unstable twist to their own destruction, as they do the other scriptures." Did you get that? Peter, *the apostle*, thought that parts of the Bible were difficult to understand. It turns out that regular ol' people like you and me are in good company.

I'll be the first to admit, Bible study is hard, y'all. It takes time, consistency, effort, and heart. But for every verse, chapter, or story that is complicated and confusing, entrenched in cultural nuances, historic specifics, and theological mind benders, there are hundreds of verses, chapters, and stories that can immediately bear weight on your life *right now*. Clear. Concise. Specific. No explanation needed.

> *For God so loved the world, that he gave his only Son, that whoever believes in him should not perish but have eternal life.*
>
> —John 3:16

> *Jesus said to him, "I am the way, and the truth, and the life. No one comes to the Father except through me."*
>
> —John 14:6

> *[F]or all have sinned and fall short of the glory of God.*
>
> —Romans 3:23

> *[D]o not be anxious about anything, but in everything by prayer and supplication with thanksgiving let your requests be made known to God.*
>
> —Philippians 4:6

See what I mean? Clear. Concise. Specific. No explanation needed. God's word speaks to you right where you are, no matter where that may be.

Before we dive into a process for Bible study, which we'll get into in chapter 7, I thought it would be helpful to provide you with some perspective. Some sturdy theological groundwork upon which you can begin building your understanding of the Bible. This chapter discusses everything I wish I had known about the Bible before I even began studying it. The following principles will change the way you approach Bible study by widening your view of God's word and rightly orienting yourself to it.

## Finding Your Footing

### 1. The Bible is a book about God.

The first thing I wish I had understood about the Bible when I initially began studying it is this: The Bible is a book about God. This one truth, more than any other Bible study tip I have ever received, absolutely revolutionized my understanding of the Bible.

As blazingly obvious as it may seem, I've found that it is something we often miss, skip over, or underemphasize, so I'll repeat it once more: *The Bible is a book about God.* As popular a notion as it may currently be, the Bible is not a book about morality, self-improvement, or living well. It may speak to these things, but to make it about those things is to devalue and trivialize it.

The point of the Bible is God Himself, with the central character of the Bible being Jesus, God in human form—the Word who "became flesh and dwelt among us" in order that we may see His glory and have access to a clear and understandable picture of who God is (John 1:14, 14:9). In John 5:39–40, Jesus reveals to us the plot and point of the Bible when He says, "You search the Scriptures because you think that in them you have eternal life; and it is they that bear witness about me, yet you refuse to come to me that you may have life." Jesus's point is this: If we read the Bible looking for anything other than Jesus, we miss the point. The purpose of the entire book is to *prepare us for* and *point us to Him.*

The Old Testament does this by predicting His coming, molding our expectations and understanding of what He will do, and setting the stage for His birth.

The New Testament does this by telling the story of His arrival and His work to bring salvation to a fallen world.

As those who study the Bible, we must be intentional in keeping the point of the Bible at the center of our study. Every book, every story, every character and every event in the Bible reveals information regarding the nature and character of God, and we study the Bible seeking out these truths. We do this by constantly asking ourselves questions such as these when we study: What does this book, story, character, or event teach me about who God is and what He does?

When you enter into Bible study looking expectantly for God, you will find Him with each turn of the page.

> *The fear of the Lord is the beginning of wisdom, and the knowledge of the Holy One is insight.*
> —Proverbs 9:10

## 2. The Bible is not a book about you.

A necessary corollary of the first point—that the Bible is a book about God—is that the Bible is *not* a book about you. Since the Bible isn't a book about you (or me), we shouldn't treat it as if it is. That means that we shouldn't read it intently focused on improving *our* lives, *our* relationships, *our* finances, *our*selves, and so on. When we read the Bible with this as our goal, we are making it a book about us. In effect, we are making ourselves the point of the Bible, which sounds pretty self-absorbed, if you stop and think about it.

Yet this is the exact framework through which most of us have been taught to view the Bible, as if this divinely inspired autobiography were really nothing more than a self-help book of sorts. As a result, we have made the Bible a book of morality tales in which we take on the lead role in every story.

- We are Abraham, diligently obeying God and then faithfully waiting on God as we persevere to get our just due.
- We are Joseph, rising above injustice and hardships to overcome and conquer.
- We are David, slaying whatever giants may stand between us and our personal achievements.

On all these accounts, we are wrong. When we enter into a study of scripture, mistakenly believing it is about us, we end up bending and twisting it so it accomplishes that very purpose. This faulty view of the Bible causes us to misuse and misunderstand the intended meaning of any given portion of scripture.

Contrary to popular belief, the purpose of the above Old Testament stories isn't to cheer us on toward self-actualization, nor is it to promote such worthy personal characteristics as perseverance, determination, and grit. The purpose of all these stories is to reveal to us something about Jesus. Humans are egocentric by nature, but the Bible remains steadfastly Christ-centric. When we read the Bible, understanding that it is about Him, not us, we begin to see more clearly. Tim Keller lays out for us to whom these Biblical characters actually point:

- ❧ Jesus is the greater Abraham, who recklessly answered God's call to leave behind all that was comfortable and familiar so that a new work could be accomplished.

- ❧ Jesus is the greater Joseph, sitting at the right hand of the king, who forgives the very ones who betrayed Him and then uses His power to save them from certain destruction.

- ❧ Jesus is the greater David, whose victory becomes His people's victory, though they were absolutely powerless to accomplish it themselves.[4]

As you can see, when we place ourselves at the center of the Bible, we narrow the scope of the Biblical narrative tragically.

Don't get me wrong, we will learn a lot about who we are as individuals, as well as human nature in general, through the study of the scriptures. However, that will look drastically different than what many of us have been trained to expect. The extent to which the Bible is about us is this: It reveals to us the truth of our sinful humanity. We identify with these big-name Biblical characters in their weaknesses and shortcomings as fallen people living in a fallen world.

- ❧ We *are* Abraham, faithless time and again, even after knowing firsthand the faithfulness of the God we serve.

- ❧ We *are* Joseph, unable to control the unforeseen twists and turns of life.

---

4. Justin Taylor, "The Bible Is Not Basically about You, *The Gospel Coalition*, accessed February 17, 2018, https://blogs.thegospelcoalition.org/justintaylor/2010/08/26/the-bible-is-not-basically-about-you/.

⚖ We *are* David, sinners woefully overcome by our mistakes and in desperate need of God's salvation.

When we look at these characters in the correct light, we see ourselves in their weaknesses and failings, and we see Christ in their glories and triumphs. What we learn about ourselves through Bible study is secondary to what we learn about God. As Jen Wilkin writes, "We must first ask, 'What does this passage teach me about God?' before we ask it to teach us anything about ourselves."[5] The Bible is not a book about you and me. It is about so much more.

### 3. The Bible tells one big story.

The Bible tells the most amazing story of all time. The point of the entire Bible is to tell this *one* story. Even though the Bible is composed of many books written by many people over a period of many hundreds of years, the theme of this *one* story is unmistakable, and there is one consistent message from God to us. There are numerous scholarly books written on this very topic, but I like the simplicity with which Sally Lloyd-Jones explains it in *The Jesus Storybook Bible*, which I read with my boys at bedtime. She explains:

> *The Bible is most of all a Story. It's an adventure story about a young Hero who comes from a far country to win back his lost treasure. It's a love story about a brave Prince who leaves his palace, his throne—everything—to rescue the one he loves....There are lots of stories in the Bible, but all the stories are telling one Big Story. The Story of how God loves his children and comes to rescue them.[6]*

5. Jen Wilkin, *Women of the Word: How to Study the Bible with Both Our Hearts and Our Minds* (Wheaton, IL: Crossway, 2014), 27.

6. Sally Lloyd-Jones, *The Jesus Storybook Bible: Every Story Whispers His Name* (Grand Rapids, MI: Zondervan, 2007), 17.

Having an understanding of the grand-scale Biblical narrative is crucial to a proper understanding of each individual character, book, story, and event within the Bible. If we isolate the different parts of the Bible, treating them as if they have no real connection to each other or to the greater plot line of the Bible as a whole, then we quickly lose our footing as we read. But when we begin to understand the Bible as one cohesive story, the themes of that story become apparent within the individual segments of the Bible. To understand the Bible correctly, we must study each portion of the Bible in light of the bigger story in which it is embedded.

The first chapter of Ephesians beautifully encapsulates for us this big-picture narrative of the Bible.

> *Blessed be the God and Father of our Lord Jesus Christ, who has blessed us in Christ with every spiritual blessing in the heavenly places, even as he chose us in him before the foundation of the world, that we should be holy and blameless before him. In love he predestined us for adoption to himself as sons through Jesus Christ, according to the purpose of his will, to the praise of his glorious grace, with which he has blessed us in the Beloved. In him we have redemption through his blood, the forgiveness of our trespasses, according to the riches of his grace, which he lavished upon us, in all wisdom and insight making known to us the mystery of his will, according to his purpose, which he set forth in Christ as a plan for the fullness of time, to unite all things in him, things in heaven and things on earth.*
>
> —Ephesians 1:3–10

Those verses paint the backdrop against which every single thing in the Bible takes place—a story in which humanity falls away from God and His perfect plan; a story in which God responds to humanity's fall by setting forth a plan to restore us back to Him in perfect relationship and unhindered fellowship. We must understand this story as a whole to more appropriately appreciate each of its individual parts. Yes, independent chapters, verses, characters, and stories will speak to you in and of themselves, but stepping back from time to time to marvel at the beauty of the entire biblical landscape will absolutely change the way you experience the Bible.

### 4. The Bible is about real people.

The stories we read about in the Bible are true stories that happened to real people. These stories reveal to us information about an *actual, living God.* I've often noticed that we tend to distance ourselves from the people, places, and happenings in the Bible by focusing on all the ways that the people are different from us, the places are unfamiliar to us, and the daily concerns and realities of life during biblical times are unrelated to us. Perhaps we picture Abraham as an unfathomably old man with a long flowing beard, David as an untouchable Renaissance man who wrestles a bear with one arm while plying a lyre with the other, and Rahab as an exotic woman of unparalleled beauty. These images are so far from the experiences of our everyday lives that it becomes easy to dismiss them as irrelevant. However, the people, places, and concerns of the Bible are altogether relevant to us. Part of our job as those who study the Bible is to find out how.

Abraham is a wanderer desperately chasing after his God-given dreams. David is a young man following God's call despite the many and profound obstacles in his way. Rahab is a woman fighting to distinguish the truth from lies. To the extent that we can, we want to step into these stories and walk around in these people's shoes, looking at the world from their perspective and thus learning about the nature and character of God right alongside them. When we do this, it becomes easier to recognize the present-tense reality of God's word being spoken to us *now* through these characters and through their stories.

## 5. The Bible is a supernatural book.

Although written by human hands, the words of the Bible are divinely inspired, with authorship of the book ultimately being attributed to God. God closely associates Himself with His word and has inextricably bound Himself to it, so much so that in the book of John, Jesus is quite simply described as "the Word."

> *In the beginning was the Word, and the Word was with God, and the Word was God.*
> —John 1:1

> *And the Word became flesh and dwelt among us.*
> —John 1:14

While this may be difficult to wrap our heads around theologically, what we can know is this: The words of the Bible possess the same qualities as their author. They are living and active, eternal, infallible, inerrant, and authoritative. Scripture is in no way reluctant to proclaim this:

> *For the word of the Lord is right and true; he is faithful in all he does.*
> —Psalm 33:4 NIV

> *Your word, Lord, is eternal; it stands firm in the heavens.*
> —Psalm 119:89 NIV

> *Every word of God is flawless.*
> —Proverbs 30:5 NIV

Just as we can trust our eternal, infallible, inerrant, and authoritative God, we can trust His eternal, infallible, inerrant, and authoritative word. We need to know this going into Bible study or we will be prone to disregard, toss aside, or pick through the segments of scripture that are more difficult to understand or believe to be true. As we've already discussed, we approach the living word of God with humility, taking great care to place ourselves in submission under it instead of lording ourselves in authority over it. His word bears weight on us, not the other way around.

Because the Bible is no ordinary book, we cannot expect to understand it through any ordinary means. As A.W. Tozer said, "The Bible is a supernatural book and can be understood only by supernatural aid."[7] We are dependent on the Holy Spirit in our study of God's word, but perhaps not in the way you might think. John Piper explains the role of the Spirit in our study of scripture:

> *The work of the Spirit is not to tell us what the manual of operation [Bible] means. That we must determine by a disciplined study of the text. The Spirit inspired these writings and he does not short-circuit them by whispering in our ear what they mean. When we pray for his help, we do not pray that he will spare us the hard work of rigorous reading and reflection. What we pray is that he would make us humble enough to welcome the truth. The work of the Spirit in helping us grasp the meaning of Christ's*

---

7. A.W. Tozer, *Fiery Faith: Ignite Your Passion for God* (Camp Hill, PA: Wing Spread Publishers, 2012).

*manual of operation [the Bible] is not to make study unnecessary but to make us radically open to receive what our study turns up, instead of twisting the text to justify our unwillingness to accept it.*[8]

We use the minds God gave us to study, explore, and press into God's word so we can comprehend it, and then we wholly depend on the Spirit to lead us to trust it, accept it, and walk in it. Here are a few verses you can use to pray as you prepare to follow where the Spirit leads in your study of God's word.

- Open my eyes, that I may behold wondrous things out of your law (Ps. 119:18).

- [T]hat the God of our Lord Jesus Christ, the Father of glory, may give you the Spirit of wisdom and of revelation in the knowledge of him (Eph. 1:17).

- Your word is a lamp to my feet and a light to my path (Ps. 119:105).

- [L]est they should see with their eyes and hear with their ears and understand with their heart and turn, and I would heal them (Matt. 13:15).

*Now we have received not the spirit of the world, but the Spirit who is from God, that we might understand the things freely given us by God.*

—1 Corinthians 2:12

---

8. John Piper, "How the Spirit Helps Us Understand," May 20, 1984, *Desiring God,* accessed February 18, 2018, http://www.desiringgod.org/messages/how-the-spirit-helps-us-understand.

## Some Solid Ground

The more I study the Bible, the more material I discover to add to the growing list of foundations. But coming to understand these five principles has completely changed the way I read my Bible. As you study, keep these foundations firmly underfoot. Allow them to shape and mold your understanding of what you read.

1. The Bible is a book about God.
2. The Bible is not a book about you.
3. The Bible tells one big story.
4. The Bible is about real people.
5. The Bible is a supernatural book.

These principles have corrected my preconceived or wrongly taught notions regarding who and what the Bible is mainly about. They have opened my eyes to the relevancy of the Bible to my life as a stay-at-home mom in the suburbs of Houston, Texas. They have given me a solid framework from which to approach my study of God's word. But most of all, they have convinced me that I can absolutely understand the Bible on my own.

The Bible is a living and active word that makes known to us a living and active God who desires that we actively come to know Him by studying His word. Jesus asserted that in searching the scriptures *we would find Him* (John 5:39). Bible study is not some cosmic game of hide-and-seek in which God aims to go undetected. Quite to the contrary. If His glory is declared by the heavens and His handiwork proclaimed by the sky (Psalm 19:1), then how much more does He make Himself known by the very words of His mouth? Seek the scriptures, my friend, so you may find Him. You've got the right perspective for study, now let's discuss a good process of study.

## Chapter 6: Dig in Deeper
Questions for Study and Reflection

1. Mark the conditions below that you feel contribute to any difficulty you experience in understanding the Bible. If there is anything other than something I have listed below, please feel free to add to my list.

   ❧ Level of education

   ❧ Intellectual ability

   ❧ Cultural background

   ❧ Religious upbringing

2. Explain how you believe any of the things you marked have inhibited your ability in the past to read and understand scripture.

3. Pick a verse below (or one of your own choosing) that specifically speaks to any fear you may have regarding your inability to understand scripture. Memorize it. Each time you study the Bible, use the verse to combat your fear.

   ❧ Isaiah 55:10–11 – For as the rain and the snow come down from heaven and do not return there but water the earth, making it bring forth and sprout, giving seed to the sower and bread to the eater, so shall my word be that goes out from my mouth; it shall not return to me empty, but it shall accomplish that which I purpose, and shall succeed in the thing for which I sent it.

   ❧ 1 Corinthians 14:33 – For God is not a God of confusion, but of peace.

❧ Psalm 19:7–9 – The law of the Lord is perfect, reviving the soul; the testimony of the Lord is sure, making wise the simple; the precepts of the Lord are right, rejoicing the heart; the commandment of the Lord is pure, enlightening the eyes; the fear of the Lord is clean, enduring forever; the rules of the Lord are true, and righteous altogether.

❧ Psalm 119:130 – The unfolding of your words gives light; it imparts understanding to the simple.

# Chapter 7: A Good Process

*In fact, though by this time you ought to be teachers, you need someone to teach you the elementary truths of God's word all over again. You need milk, not solid food! Anyone who lives on milk, being still an infant, is not acquainted with the teaching about righteousness. But solid food is for the mature, who by constant use have trained themselves to distinguish good from evil.*

—Hebrews 5:12–14 NIV

The above verses from the book of Hebrews epitomizes the place I found myself many years after becoming a Christian—still dependent on other people to feed me the truths of the Bible. It was not because I was incapable of feeding myself, but because I lacked the confidence to pick up the metaphorical spoon and try.

*Bible literacy is a necessary component of the Christian life.* We cannot have access to the Bible, choose *not* to study it, and still insist on our identity as a believer of Christ—not when Jesus so emphatically contended otherwise. "Man shall not live by bread alone, but by every word that comes from the mouth of God" (Matt. 4:4). Maybe like me, you've found yourself at a place where you've grown weary of staring at the spoon, insisting that it's entirely too complicated of a contraption for you to use. This chapter is for those of you who are ready to pick up the spoon and give it a try. It's for those of you who are eager to feed on God's word, allowing it to grow you out of spiritual infancy and into spiritual maturity.

Growth, in all instances, involves a process, a systematic series of actions directed to some end. Infusing a process that is both *practical* and *purposeful* into your Bible study will put you in the position for that growth to occur. Let's look at the ways in which you can study both practically and purposefully so we can muster up the courage to give that spoon a try.

**Study Practically**
To begin, let's get practical. If the Bible study system we put into place isn't practical, it won't last long. Above all else, I've found that practicality promotes endurance when it comes to Bible study. As we set out to make individual Bible study part of our day-to-day living, we want to ensure success in our endeavors. To do this, we must talk matters of practicality. Specifically, when, where, and what are you going to study?

### The when and the where

If you don't have a plan for when and where you're going to sit down and consistently study the Bible, you're never going to consistently study the Bible. However, that is exactly where your growth is going to occur—in your *consistent* and *frequent* study of the Bible. Just as you wouldn't choose to occasionally feed a young child and expect that child to remain healthy, you can't expect to grow into spiritual maturity by occasionally picking up your Bible. We must be consistent and frequent in our study of the Bible.

Take a look at what the Apostle Paul had to say concerning the people of Berea:

> *Now these Jews were more noble than those in Thessalonica; they received the word with all eagerness, examining the Scriptures daily to see if these things were so.*
>
> —Acts 17:11

Did you catch that? Paul, who was not an easy guy to impress, by the way, was struck by the way the Bereans searched the scriptures *daily*. It was through their daily and consistent study of God's word that they were able to test what was being taught contrary to God's word. This is one of the reasons we, too, must consistently study the Bible—primarily to come to know God, yes, but the flip side of that is understanding what is *not* God. Recognizing who God *isn't* is a big part of coming to recognize who God *is*. Coming to know someone with this degree of confidence takes commitment and consistency, so your Bible study is going to need both.

That is why the first step in studying the Bible is both the easiest to set forth and the one most guaranteed to bring you success: commit to a specific time and place for your study. That's it! If you can do this one thing and follow through, you're well on your way to becoming a Bible pro.

In chapter 3, I gave you a glimpse of what the when and where of Bible study looks like for me, but you do what works for *you*. Early morning before the family wakes up? During your lunch hour? Last thing at night before you settle in for bed? There's no wrong time or place. As long as you're specific and consistent, you're good.

When I taught at a university in downtown Houston, I would get to work early before the parking garage reached capacity and then sit in my car and do Bible study before going in to teach. I can still recall the exact verses I memorized sitting in that garage. That worked well for a season, and when my schedule changed, I changed my Bible study to fit it.

Just as the when and where of your Bible study will change from time to time, the amount of time you spend studying daily will likely fluctuate as well. I am *not* going to tell you how long you need to study each day. You can faithfully pursue God through His word for 10 minutes a day. You can faithfully pursue God through His word for an hour each day. How much time you spend is not as important as the consistency with which you spend it. One of the constant battles we must guard against is the tendency for us to drift toward legalism in our study of God's word. The minute we become legalistic in our attempts to meet God in His word, we need to go back and begin again by searching out our motivations.

## The what

So you know when and where you'll be reading, but *what* will you read? The obvious answer is the Bible, but if you've attempted Bible study before, you may have noticed that there are a lot of different choices when it comes to Bible selection. That has to do with the way in which the Bible is translated from its original languages into English.

Some translations—English Standard Version (ESV), King James Version (KJV), New American Standard Bible (NASB)—attempt to keep the exact words and phrases of the original text intact. These are known as literal, or word-for-word, translations. Other translations, most popularly the New International Version (NIV), translate the original language into English thought by thought.

These translations tend to be easier to read and understand. Still other translations, such as The Message, are known as paraphrases. Paraphrased translations seek to convey the ideas of the original text without being constrained by the original language or grammar.

The translation you choose can greatly impact your ability to read and comprehend the Bible, so spend some time comparing different versions. My personal preference for several years has been the ESV, but I read and studied the NIV for years before that. I know many prefer the KJV for scripture memorization because the translation does a good job of keeping the poetic aspect of the text. It might also make sense to choose the version your church uses.

The point is, we are fortunate to have many good and reliable translations available to choose from. My suggestion is to pick either a word-for-word or thought-by-thought translation that reads easily to you. Reserve the paraphrased versions more for commentary and less for your individual daily study since these translations insert a lot of the translator's thoughts and ideas into the translation process. The good news is that no matter the translation you choose, all translations are available online for you to compare and contrast, and to aid in your understanding of a particular passage. Websites such as biblegateway.com even allow you to open the same verse in multiple translations at the same time.

Other than a Bible, it will be helpful to have the following supplies on hand. Feel free to totally geek out if you're an office supply junkie like I am. I've constrained myself to the bare minimum to keep this system accessible and easy to use, but I'm as susceptible to the allure of a big pack of pastel colored Post-its as the next person, and my Bible is full of them. Don't you dare let anyone rain on your Bible-study-office-supply parade. Go big here if that's your style. Celebrate the beginning of each new study with new supplies to match. You've earned it. Just make sure to include the following:

- Something to write with. A pencil or pen will suffice, but if colored pencils, highlighters, and markers are your jam, then go with it.

- Something to write in. I'm a spiral-bound notebook kind of gal myself, but you can get as fancy as you want here—a real leather journal, an old-school trapper keeper, or a Lisa Frank three-ring binder could totally rock your Bible study.

- A Bible concordance. Don't worry, there's an app for that. A concordance contains an alphabetical index of words used in the Bible and the main Bible references where the word occurs. It is an extremely easy and useful Bible study tool. You can find these free online or as an app for your smartphone. I use the Strong's Concordance app on my iPhone.

- Several versions of the Bible. You don't need to own print copies. Just hop online to access every version in existence. My go-to site for this is biblegateway.com.

**Study Purposefully**

Now that we've gathered our supplies and determined the time and place of our study, we get to move on to the most exciting part of all—actually *reading* the Bible. Many attempts at Bible study dwindle quickly because we don't enter into this part of the process purposefully. Instead, we randomly enter into Bible study by simply flipping around until we find a page to read. This approach is much like taking a shot in the dark. Chances are, we're going to miss our target.

To achieve the desired outcome of actually understanding what we read, we must carefully take aim. To do that, we're going to need a plan. The goal of the Bible study method I detail below is to infuse *purpose* and a clearly defined *process* into your study. As I've stated from the outset, this method of Bible study is aimed to be simple to follow, but effective in practice.

Step 1:  Pick a book of the Bible.
Step 2:  Study the context of the book.
Step 3:  Read the book.
Step 4:  Respond to God's word.
Step 5:  Be changed by God's word.

My hope is that these five steps provide you with an easy-to-follow guide and will lead you through your individual study of the Bible. In no way do I desire to take *you* out of your study of the Bible. Remember, *you* are the one doing the work. *You* are the one digging deeply into scripture. This process can help guide you through your study, but it cannot study for you. For this or any method to work, you must own your study of the Bible.

Now that you have an idea of what you're getting into, let's go over it together, one step at a time.

## Step 1: Pick a book of the Bible

Steps 1 and 2 of this Bible study process are what my friend Melanie refers to as the pre-study study. In other words, it's the studying you have to do before you are able to study the Bible well.

Without a doubt, Step 1 is the most difficult part of the Bible study process for me. Chalk it up to a fear of commitment, but choosing which book of the Bible I'm going to study and then staying with that book until the very last page is always a tough decision for me to make. I always begin reading a book with all the best intentions to see that book through, but then I get distracted by what a friend may be studying at the time (*Oh, she seems to be getting so much out of that book!*) or by the latest study my favorite teacher published. (*Dang it! That's what I should have chosen to study next!*) But commitment is the key. Fight the inevitable battle of Bible study envy and be faithful to the book at hand. The first step of effective Bible study is to pick a book of the Bible and then stick with it.

Studying the Bible book by book is a sure way to begin increasing your Bible literacy. Because the Bible was written book by book, it is best understood this way, with each book being a cohesive and easily defined unit of study unto itself.

One of the greatest benefits of a book-by-book method of Bible study is that it helps us avoid taking verses and teachings out of context since the book provides the context. For instance, one of the most well-known, greatly loved, and oft-quoted verses of the Bible is Jeremiah 29:11 — "For I know the plans I have for you, declares the Lord, plans for welfare and not for evil, to give you a future and a hope." People tend to love this verse because it sounds so dang optimistic, but if you understand the context of the verse, the meaning goes well beyond mere optimism.

As you read the book of Jeremiah from beginning to end, you'll pick up on the following information before you come to that particular verse. Jeremiah was a prophet to Israel (really just the nation of Judah at that point) during a time of great rebellion. The people had grown prideful and idolatrous and were no longer obeying God. Part of God's plan for restoring them back to Himself, back to "a future and a hope" was to send them into captivity and exile by way of the Babylonians. This burden of captivity would reawaken them to the goodness and faithfulness of their God. They would recognize their idolatry and return to God, broken and repentant. When you read this verse in context, the meaning becomes clear:

> For thus says the LORD: When seventy years are completed for Babylon, I will visit you, and I will fulfill to you my promise and bring you back to this place. For I know the plans I have for you, declares the LORD, plans for welfare and not for evil, to give you a future and a hope. Then you will call upon me and come and pray to me, and I will hear you. You will seek me and find me, when you seek me with all your heart. I will be found by you, declares the LORD, and I will restore your fortunes and gather you from all the nations and all the places where I have driven you, declares the LORD, and I will bring you back to the place from which I sent you into exile.
>
> —Jeremiah 29:10–14

Understanding Jeremiah 29:11 in its context completely transforms its meaning. It's no longer a shallow verse that speaks of some vague good plan for your life. It gives us great insight into God's faithful character and devotion to His people. You begin to see the Bible for what it truly is—not just some book filled with flimsy promises that don't really hold up under the hardships of real life, but a book that tells of a good and mighty God who is working desperately through any and all circumstances to bring a rebellious people back to Himself. Studying the Bible book by book keeps us from making the Bible less than it is. It allows God's word to speak to us instead of allowing us to tell the Bible what we want or need it to say.

A book-by-book study of the Bible is definitely the way to go. However, the question still remains: *How do I know which book to study first, or second, third, or fourth?* My best advice to you here is this: set yourself up for success. I learned this the hard way. You want to know the first book of the Bible this overachiever set out to diligently study? Isaiah! At 66 chapters long and chock-full of messianic prophecy, Isaianic oracles (I know, right?), and a complicated historical backdrop, the book of Isaiah is not the best place to cut your Bible study teeth. I gave it a heartfelt go, tried my best to impress myself, and failed pretty quickly. But it was a lesson well learned. Give your knowledge and understanding of the Bible time to grow upon itself.

That being said, a great place to begin your understanding of the Bible is somewhere in the Gospel accounts of the New Testament. Matthew, Mark, Luke, and John all tell the story of Jesus's earthly ministry. Each of those books is directed to a different audience and stress different themes of Jesus's ministry and aspects of His character. The Gospels are our most significant source of information on Jesus, so you can't go wrong by beginning with one of them. The book of Mark is fast-paced, easy to read, and a short 16 chapters long. That would be an excellent place to start.

After you tackle one or more of the Gospels, I encourage you to try your hand at the Old Testament as well. You could even intersperse your reading of the New Testament Gospels with the first five books of the Old Testament, like this—Mark, *Genesis*, John, *Exodus*, Matthew, *Leviticus*, Luke, *Numbers*, Acts (not one of the Gospels but in many ways a continuation of the book of Luke), *Deuteronomy*. By the time you work your way through these 10 books, you will have given yourself a solid foundation upon which to grow even further. Another idea is to commit to studying whatever book your church is going through at the time. These are just a few suggestions to get you thinking, but there is no shortage of opinions on this topic, and there is really no wrong answer (except for Isaiah; definitely don't begin with Isaiah).

Although we may stumble upon great truths in God's word through any method of study, we have the greatest chance of correctly understanding God's meaning when we study God's word in its correct context. Studying the Bible book by book is a good way to help assure that you do this. That is how you build a foundational understanding of the entire Bible. Context plays a huge role in gaining Bible literacy, as Step 2 will reveal in even greater detail.

## Step 2: Study the context of the book

Step 2 is your last step of pre-study study before you get to dive into the actual text of the Bible. The work you put in here will pay off in huge dividends when you continue on to Step 3.

Rarely, if ever, do I begin reading any book by turning immediately to its first page. I generally begin by doing some investigative work. I read the author's bio on the inside jacket of the book. Who are they? What is their background, and where are they from? What else have they written? What authority do they have on the topic at hand? I also like to read the reviews of the book and the author, both praise and criticism. I flip to the back cover and read the synopsis of the book. Who are the main characters? What is the main plot of the story? What kind of book is it? Is there anything I need to know going in? This is the way many of us approach reading new material. So why should we approach the Bible any differently? We shouldn't.

The second step of effective Bible study is to explore the context of the book. Before you get overwhelmed by the potential amount of work this step could require, know this: I'm going to outline for you the exact questions you need to ask in order to explore the book's context *and* I'm going to tell you exactly where you can find that information. Hang in there as you work your way through this step. There's a light at the end of this tunnel.

Step 2 is essential because understanding the basic information surrounding the circumstances of each book will help you correctly approach your reading, comprehension, and application of that book. It will also assist you in correctly placing that particular book within the greater context of the Bible as a whole. The questions you need to answer regarding a book's context are straightforward and direct, and should take you right back to your days in high school English (you're welcome for this): who, what, when, where, and why.

**Who?** *Who wrote the book?* Because God used human authors to write down His holy word, *Who?* is a very important question to ask. Knowing the author from the get-go gives us immediate insight into the book. Although every biblical author is speaking the inspired word of God, each one does so in his own voice and with his own style. Paul reads much differently than Luke and Moses much differently than David. God used the individual personalities, backgrounds, and experiences of the human authors of the Bible to influence the way the book was written and, as a result, the way each book should be read. This was His design in writing the Bible the way He did. We should seek out the distinctive characteristics of each biblical author.

*Who is the book written to?* Did the author of the book personally know the people or person to whom the book was written? What was the relationship between them? Think about how the relationship you share with someone influences the tone with which you speak to them and the things you can or cannot say to them. To make sense of what the book is supposed to mean to us, we must first make sense of what the book meant to its original audience.

*Who is the book written about?* Is there a main character at the center of the action of the particular book you are studying? If so, take note. Jot down what you learn about this person as you read and study.

**What?** The Bible as a whole is categorized as a work of literature, yet each book of the Bible is categorized under varying types of literature. The type of literature greatly impacts the way that book is meant to be read. You'll want to know what type, or genre, of literature you're reading because that will determine how you handle the text. For instance, we expect and allow a poet to write differently than a historian. Below are the genres of literature found in the Bible as well as a chart detailing which book belongs to which genre (this time, you're really welcome).

- *Is it law?* These books are meant to define the proper relationship between God and humans, humans among themselves, and humans to the world in general. The books of the Law help establish God's expectations for us.

- *Is it history?* Many of the books of the Bible include some history, but the historical books of the Bible are focused on history. They should be read the same way you would read any other work of historical nonfiction. They inform us of particular people, places, and times within the biblical narrative and should be read as the factual retelling of events.

- *Is it wisdom literature?* This genre is comprised of concise sayings meant to impart wisdom and give instruction regarding how to live and the meaning of life. These are meant to convey principles that are generally true, but not necessarily universally so.

- *Is it poetry?* The poetic books use all manner of literary devices that we must take into account when interpreting them. Metaphors, similes, symbolism, and parallelism are all commonly used in this genre. Because poetry is more difficult to translate than other types of literature, we lose some of the poetic intent during the translation process.

- *Is it a Gospel narrative?* The New Testament Gospels are among the narrative accounts of the Bible. The Gospels are specifically biographical narratives about Jesus. A narrative is a structured story told by a narrator. It has a plot, a setting, characters, and themes.

- *Is it an epistle?* The epistles refer to the 21 letters in the New Testament. The apostles wrote these letters to individuals or churches. They include instruction, rebuke, correction, and explanation. As with most letters, there is a degree of familiarity between the writer and the recipient. To understand the letters, we need to know the circumstances under which they were written.

- *Is it prophecy?* The prophetic books of the Old Testament made predictions of Israel's future and gave warnings based on those predictions. They serve/ served as an opportunity for us/them to recognize sin and turn toward repentance and obedience.

- *Is it apocalyptic literature?* This is a specific form of prophecy that tells us of events still yet to occur. There is a great use of symbolism and imagery involved in this type of writing.

Notice that books of the Bible can also be combinations of any of the above genres. For instance, the book of Judges is primarily historical; however, chapter 5 is a song, or poem, of Deborah. The books that Moses authored contain both law and history, as well as some poetry. The book of Daniel is both historical and prophetic. As you read, these shifts in genre will often be apparent, and you'll want to change your reading and understanding of the text to match the genre of the writing. Use the chart below to help you quickly determine which type of literary genre the book you are reading fits into most closely.

## Books of the Bible by Literary Genre

| Genre | Books |
|---|---|
| Law | Exodus, Leviticus, Numbers, Deuteronomy |
| History | Genesis, Joshua, Judges, Ruth, 1 and 2 Samuel, 1 and 2 Kings, 1 and 2 Chronicles, Ezra, Nehemiah, Esther, Acts (church history) |
| Wisdom Literature | Job, Proverbs, Ecclesiastes |
| Poetry | Psalms, Song of Solomon, Lamentations |
| Gospel Narrative | Matthew, Mark, Luke, John |
| Epistle | Romans, 1 and 2 Corinthians, Galatians, Ephesians, Philippians, Colossians, 1 and 2 Thessalonians, 1 and 2 Timothy, Titus, Philemon, Hebrews, James, 1 and 2 Peter, 1, 2, and 3 John, Jude |
| Prophecy | Isaiah, Jeremiah, Ezekiel, Daniel, Hosea, Joel, Amos, Obadiah, Jonah, Micah, Nahum, Habakkuk, Zephaniah, Haggai, Zechariah, Malachi |
| Apocalyptic Literature | Daniel, Revelation |

I know Step 2 is a doozy, and charts can be distracting, so in case you've forgotten, we're studying the context of our book. We've covered the *who* and the *what*. Now let's go on to the *when*, the *where*, and the *why*. I promise you, this next part will fly by.

**When and where?** *When was the book written? Where was it written?* Knowing the time and place in which a book was written gives us the correct historical context from which to understand and interpret the author's words. Knowing the *when* and *where* will point us to the cultural assumptions, customs, and traditions of the time. It will give us insight into how the world worked when the book was written; what the roles of men, women, and children were at the time; and how varying groups of people were perceived and treated. It will also clue us in to any significant historical events that may have been influencing the author at the time. Not just knowing, but rather *investigating,* the timeframe of a book's writing will greatly aid in your understanding of the book and help you correctly place the book within the entire biblical storyline.

**Why?** *Why was this book written?* Answering that question reveals the purpose the author had in writing the book in the first place. It also enlightens us as to what impact the author hoped the book would have on his audience. Was it primarily written to encourage? To correct? To inform? Was the book intended to be a response to any particular happening or set of circumstances? If so, we want to know all of this going into our study of the book.

There you have it. Everything you need to know about the context of the book in a pre-cracked nutshell. I'm sure you can recognize the benefits of knowing the *who, what, when, where,* and *why* of the book you're studying. Perhaps you're wondering how on earth you're supposed to figure all these answers out. So why don't I just go ahead and tell you?

Once you begin reading the biblical book you've chosen, I'll ask you to put aside outside resources for a bit. However, in researching the context of the book, I encourage you to use such resources. You can find information on the context of your book in any good biblical commentary as well as in several trusted online resources (I like blueletterbible.org.) Perhaps most convenient, your very own Bible most likely contains this information. Many Bibles, especially a good study Bible, will detail the context of each book. For instance, my ESV journaling Bible contains a section at the end where it introduces each book of the Bible. Before I begin a study of any one book (take John, for instance), I can turn in my Bible to the section of introductions and easily discover the following:

## Context of the Book of John

### Who wrote it?
The apostle John

### To whom was it written?
The text doesn't explicitly say, but we do know it was written "so that you may believe" (John 20:31). Presumably, John's intended audience was young disciples of the Christian faith whom he hoped to confirm and secure in their faith.

### What type of literature is it?
Gospel narrative

### When was it written?
Approximately AD 85

### Where was it written?
We don't know where John was when he wrote this book, but we do know that the action of the story follows Jesus around during His ministry. Where Jesus was geographically located is mentioned many times throughout the book.

### Why was it written?

The purpose of this book is explicitly stated in chapter 20, verse 31: "but these are written so that you may believe that Jesus is the Christ, the Son of God, and that by believing you may have life in his name."

See? There is no need for you to reinvent the wheel as you research the context of the book. Use the information that has already been collected to your own Bible study benefit. Write down the answer to each contextual question in your notebook so you can easily refer back to it as you study. Writing it down provides the additional benefit of helping you remember it.

Once you gather this basic information, feel free to go on from there. You may want to look up the apostle John to learn more about him. Did he write any other books of the Bible? Is there anything significant about his life and ministry that can help us better understand him? You can turn to the other book introductions in your Bible to see what else was written at that same time. Or you could explore what was going on historically at the time of the book's writing. The whole point of exploring these questions is to prime yourself to better understand the book. Once you have answered as many of these questions as you can, you're finally ready to move on beyond the pre-study portion of Bible study and onto the actual study part of Bible study, which begins with reading the book.

## Step 3: Read the Book

One of the significant upsides of following this process of Bible study is that by the time you actually begin reading the book, you're already somewhat familiar with it. (Hip hip hooray! All your pre-study study has paid off!) You've had the chance to dip your feet in the water and gauge exactly what it is you're about to jump into.

You want to do your best to set yourself up for success. After you've thoughtfully chosen a book and researched its context, you're finally ready to start reading. During this stage of the process, I want you to intentionally avoid the temptation to read commentaries, study notes, or paraphrases of the text. *The goal of this method of Bible study is to put you in the position to study on your own, without the immediate aid of any supplemental materials.* You want to do your own work here.

Before you dive into the deep waters of Step 3, I want to offer some encouragement, lest you occasionally feel that you're drowning beneath a sea of Bible books, chapters, and verses. My encouragement is this: Studying the Bible is a lifetime pursuit. This is a book you will be reading *for the rest of your life.* You should not expect understanding to occur in one fell swoop, nor should you be discouraged when it does not. Every time you study another book of the Bible, you will understand the Bible more thoroughly. Each time you return to a specific book for another round, you will find something in it that you missed before.

This is one of the many beauties of God's word. Because the Bible is living and active, it possesses the ability to respond to exactly where you are right now. As your life changes, God is capable of using the same word to speak a brand new thing into your life. Understanding this, I want to stress that there are several ways you can go about learning God's word. My goal here is to give you a place to start, to help you begin the process of digging into scripture with your very own hands. So pull up your sleeves, and let's get started.

**First, read your book through once.** Begin by reading the book in its entirety. I call this the fly-over phase. You're not taking too long to look at any one thing in great detail, but you're getting a great sense of the general landscape of the book.

During this first read-through, be on the lookout for repeated words, important characters, significant events, and main themes. Take note of anything that catches your attention or any questions you have. Don't let anything trip you up for too long. Catch what you can and then move on. If the book is fairly short, it's great to be able to do this read-through in one sitting. If it's a longer book, divide it up and read it in a few days to a week, if possible. After you finish this first read-through, you should be able to answer the question *What is the book about?* in pretty general terms. Even if you can't do that, you're still okay. We'll get there. Just keep going.

**Next, take it chapter by chapter.** After completing your fly-over reading of the book, you're ready to read the book a second time, moving chapter by chapter at a much slower pace.

In chapter 6 we discussed the importance of recognizing that the entire Bible tells one big story. We can significantly improve our understanding of scripture by considering how each segment of scripture fits into the one big story the Bible is telling. We can do this by answering a handful of questions each time we read a new chapter. For the second read-through, I want you to read the book one chapter at a time, answering as many of the following questions as you can from each chapter:

Q1:  What does this passage teach me about God?
(Who is He? What is He like? What does He do?)

Q2:  What does this passage teach me about humanity?
(Who are we? What are we like? What do we do? How are we like God in each of these things? How are we unlike God in each of these things?)

Q3: What does this passage teach me about the nature of the relationship between God and humanity? (As it currently is? As it was originally designed to be?)

Q4: What truth does this passage illuminate? What lie does this passage uncover?

Q5: What conviction, correction, instruction, encouragement, or promise does this passage offer me?

That's it. Read through your daily chapter with your eyes trained on discovering the answers to these five questions, and you're uncovering a small bit of the big story of the Bible in each and every sitting. Let's give this a try to see how it works itself out in a few passages.

Read Genesis 1 from beginning to end.

Record how long it takes you to do that here: _____

(This will give you a general idea of the daily time commitment this method of study requires.)

Once you've done that, go back and read Genesis 1 again. This time, search for and record the answers to the five questions as you go along. Take notes on the page provided.

Record how long it takes you to do that here: _____

After you record your observations, take a peek at the following page to see what my notes ended up looking like.

*Genesis 1*

*Your Observations*

Q1: What does this passage teach me about God?
(Who is He? What is He like? What does He do?)

Q2: What does this passage teach me about humanity?
(Who are we? What are we like? What do we do? How
are we like God in each of these things? How are we
unlike God in each of these things?)

Q3: What does this passage teach me about the nature of the
relationship between God and humanity?
(As it currently is? As it was originally designed to be?)

Q4: What truth does this passage illuminate? What lie does
this passage uncover?

Q5: What conviction, correction, instruction, encouragement,
or promise does this passage offer me?

*Genesis 1*

*My Observations*

**Q1:** What does this passage teach me about God?
(Who is He? What is He like? What does He do?)

He creates. He is creative.

His Spirit is present.

He speaks. He sees.

He calls. He names.

What He creates is good.

He separates light from darkness and living things according to their kind.

He places things appropriately.

He blesses.

He provides.

**Q2:** What does this passage teach me about humanity?
(Who are we? What are we like? What do we do? How are we like God in each of these things? How are we unlike God in each of these things?)

We are made in His image.

We were created male and female.

He has given us dominion over all the earth.

All of God's creation was originally good.

**Q3:** What does this passage teach me about the nature of the relationship between God and humanity?
(As it currently is? As it was originally designed to be?)

God created people. God blessed people.

God initiated a relationship with people.

The relationship between God and humanity was originally good.

Q4: What truth does this passage illuminate? What lie does this passage uncover?

In the absence of God's intervention, there was void, emptiness, darkness.

After God enters, there is light, difference, separation.

What He commands comes to be. God works in an orderly fashion.

Q5: What conviction, reproof, correction, instruction, encouragement or promise does this passage offer me?

God appropriately placed the sun in the sky, and He has appropriately placed me in the exact place I am to be.

Any distance between God and me does not exist because of Him. He created me and then came near to me. I am made in His image, in His likeness.

How'd you do? Don't worry if you weren't able to pull as much out of the text as I did in my example. My notes certainly weren't that comprehensive the first time around. Perhaps you only emerged with two or three observations. You still see, know, and understand more than you did just a few minutes ago. You've made good progress.

This process builds upon itself, and the learning curve is steep at first. Do the hard work of keeping on, and you *will* begin to see and understand more. Remember, you want to allow yourself time to grow in your knowledge of scripture. You have to train your eyes to begin seeing what is there. Using these five questions to guide your reading will do just that.

Let's try it once again, this time with a New Testament passage. Apply the same process you just completed for Genesis 1 while reading John 1, verses 1–18. John 1 is a long chapter, so I broke it up. Feel free to do the same as you study on your own.

Read John 1:1–18 all the way through.

Record how long it takes you to do that here: _____

Once you've done that, go back and read it once more. This time, search for the answers to the five questions as you go along. You can mark them down on the page provided.

Record how long it takes you to do that here: _____

When you've finished, you can find my observations of the text on the page that follows.

## John 1:1–18

### Your Observations

Q1: What does this passage teach me about God?
(Who is He? What is He like? What does He do?)

Q2: What does this passage teach me about humanity?
(Who are we? What are we like? What do we do? How are we like God in each of these things? How are we unlike God in each of these things?)

Q3: What does this passage teach me about the nature of the relationship between God and humanity?
(As it currently is? As it was originally designed to be?)

Q4: What truth does this passage illuminate? What lie does this passage uncover?

Q5: What conviction, correction, instruction, encouragement, or promise does this passage offer me?

John 1:1–18

My Observations

Q1:  What does this passage teach me about God?
(Who is He? What is He like? What does He do?)

He is the Word. (The Word = God; the Word is with God.)
He has been since the beginning.
He made the world (He creates).
He possesses life. He is life.
He is light. He shines in the darkness.
He came to us. He put on flesh and came to dwell among us.
He is full of grace and truth.
Jesus makes God known. He makes God knowable.
He reveals the glory of the Father.
He is full of grace and truth.

Q2:  What does this passage teach me about humanity?
(Who are we? What are we like? What do we do? How
are we like God in each of these things? How are we
unlike God in each of these things?)

Jesus's life is our light.
Like John, we have the capacity to be His witnesses, to bear
    truth about Jesus so others may believe in Him.
We are not the light.
Many did not receive Him when He came.
Those who do receive Him become His children.
People have seen His glory.
From His fullness, we receive grace and then more grace.
We have the opportunity, like John, to bear witness about
    Jesus.

Q3: What does this passage teach me about the nature of the relationship between God and humanity?
(As it currently is? As it was originally designed to be?)

We are born His through His will alone. (I cannot do this. I cannot initiate this relationship.)
Humankind refused to receive the one who created us, but He pursues us nonetheless.

Q4: What truth does this passage illuminate? What lie does this passage uncover?

He is not a distant God. He has and continues to come near.

Q5: What conviction, reproof, correction, instruction, encouragement, or promise does this passage offer me?

I have refused (and in some ways still refuse) to receive Him.
When I do turn to Him, I receive grace upon grace.
The darkness has not overcome the light. (It cannot. It will not.)

Between those five questions, there is so much more for you uncover. And you will! As God reveals truth to you, grab hold of it and pull it near. The more you seek His word, the more understanding He will give you. Listen to what Jesus taught:

> And he said to them, "Pay attention to what you hear: with the measure you use, it will be measured to you, and still more will be added to you. For to the one who has, more will be given, and from the one who has not, even what he has will be taken away."
>
> —Mark 4:24–25

These verses are often pulled out of context and thrust into the realm of the prosperity gospel. It's a false version of the gospel that wrongfully asserts that financial wealth and physical wellness are always God's best plan for our lives. Far from having to do with material riches, these verses have to do with the riches of God's word. Once we hear the good news of the gospel, it does us little good unless we take notice of it, diligently consider it, and look into it deeply. If we make good use of the knowledge we have, no matter how little we have to begin with, God will be faithful to grow it. I like how the Amplified Bible explains this verse:

> Then He said to them, "Pay attention to what you hear. By your own standard of measurement [that is, to the extent that you study spiritual truth and apply godly wisdom] it will be measured to you [and you will be given even greater ability to respond]—and more will be given to you besides. For whoever has [a teachable

*heart], to him more [understanding] will be given; and whoever does not have [a yearning for truth], even what he has will be taken away from him."*

—Mark 4:24–25 AMP

The five questions I propose in this book are designed so you can begin working, right now, with exactly how much knowledge you have. If you've never so much as opened the Bible, these questions can guide you through. They are simple and straightforward and draw your attention to the most foundational truths of the Bible. Or perhaps like me, you've been a student of the Bible for years. These questions will direct your attention upward and out to the sweeping panoramic view of the whole of God's story. My hope is that no matter how acquainted you are with the pages of your Bible, these questions will uncover things you have yet to see.

### Step 4: Respond to God's word

By this point in the process, you have picked a book, researched the context of that book, and actually started reading it. This is huge! You are reading and understanding the Bible! *You* are actually doing this. Rock on, my friends! I knew you could do it! Now let's keep the momentum going as we go on to Step 4, which has become one of my favorite parts of Bible study.

The Bible is God's word spoken to us. One of the most important lessons I've learned in my pursuit of the Lord through the study of His word is this: *Every revelation from God requires a response from us.* (And for the record, not responding counts as a response, just probably not the type of response you want to give the sovereign God of all creation.) Relationships require that when one participant speaks, the other responds. I'm guessing you respond to your friends, your boss, your mom, or your sister when they speak to you. Likewise, we respond when the Lord is speaking to us. Our study of God's word is not complete until we do so. When we fail to respond to whatever word the Lord has spoken to us through our study of scripture, it's like dropping a call. It's short-circuiting the process of communication.

There are many ways you can choose to respond to God's word. I've cried and begged for forgiveness in response to God's word. I've whispered words of thanksgiving and gratitude. I've been moved to pray for someone the Holy Spirit brought to mind through a specific passage. In and through all this, I was responding to what God spoke to me. The more you study God's word, the more naturally you will respond in ways that feel comfortable to you. To get you started, let's look at a handful of ways we can respond to a God who speaks. The ideas I offer are not meant to constitute a systematic process for responding to God's word. You should respond as the Holy Spirit leads. But because I know the notion of responding to God's word is foreign to some people, I wanted to present options for you to explore as you set your heart on responding.

Here are some ways you can respond to Him as He speaks to you.

### Listen to His word

Listening is always your first response to God's word. We discussed listening thoroughly in chapter 3, but I want to make sure you recognize listening for what it is. Your listening, in and of itself, is evidence of a God who speaks. The fact that you listen to God speaking signifies your belief in a God who seeks fellowship and a relationship with you. This is no small thing. Listening intently puts you in the necessary position to respond even further.

## Dwell on His word

Other than listening, you respond to God by dwelling on His word. To dwell on God's word means that you linger over it, you emphasize it in your life, you ponder it in thought, speech, or writing. When you dwell on something, you allow it to take up permanent residence and reside within you. This is a good and necessary response to the word God has given us. There are so many beautiful and beneficial ways in which you can do this.

    *Dwell on God's word by memorizing it.*
As you read through the Bible chapter by chapter, take note of the verses that seem to be speaking directly to you or your situation. Look for the verses that offer you specific guidance, encouragement, or instruction. Seek out places where God reveals who He is and what He does. Write the verse on an index card. Put it in your car and look at it when you stop for a light or when you're stuck in traffic. Tape it to your bathroom mirror. Afix it to the refrigerator. Read the verse over and over again until you know it by heart.

    *Dwell on God's word by meditating on it.*
To meditate means to engage in thought, to contemplate, or to reflect on something. I know full well how tempting it can be to fly through your Bible-reading time just to get it done. Sometimes the demands and schedule of the day at hand leave no other choice. However, there is so much value in simply thinking on God's word, reading it slowly, saying it out loud, and soaking it in. Try this if you

come to a verse you simply can't comprehend. Do it also when you find a verse that truly feeds your soul.

🐦 *Dwell on God's word by writing about it.*
When I began blogging in 2014, I did so in order to record how God's word had consistently met me right where I was. Often, after reading and studying a portion of scripture, I was struck by what the Lord was saying to me through it—how He was using His word to speak to the exact place in which I found myself. I would sit and write about what He had revealed. Today, I can look back on those old entries and remind myself how faithful God has been, consistently meeting me through His word. If you enjoy writing or journaling like I do, this is a way you can dwell on God's word.

🐦 *Dwell on God's word by talking about it.*
Once a week, I conference call two of my friends who live in different cities, and we study the Bible together for about half an hour or so. Before the call, we each read the assigned chapter of the book we are studying, and then we prepare our thoughts and questions for discussion.
Each Wednesday evening, my family and I gather with other families from our church to spend some time discussing the passages that were taught at church the prior Sunday.
Talking about God's word is a worthwhile way to dwell on it. Discussion gives you an opportunity to share what the Lord is doing for you through His word as well as learn what He is doing for others through that very same text.

🐾 *Dwell on God's word by creating art inspired by it.*
I am artistically challenged. I get nervous at the thought of scrapbooking and have been known to go into a full-scale panic attack when faced with the daunting task of creating end-of-year teacher gifts. While I more easily make sense of God's word through writing about it, you may be gifted with the ability to make sense of God's word through drawing, sketching, or painting about it. Do yourself a favor and Google the words *Bible journaling*, or search those same words on Pinterest. This is a whole thing, y'all. If God has given you the desire or ability to exalt His word in this way, go for it. It is a visually stunning and impactful way to dwell on His word.

No matter how you choose to dwell on what you have read each day, the point of this step is to ingrain His word in your heart.

*Your word I have treasured and stored in my heart.*
—Psalm 119:11 AMP

**Praying over His word**
One final way you can respond to God is by praying over His word. This one thing—prayer—will increase your intimacy and closeness to the Lord more than any other thing you can do. I cannot overemphasize the longing of God's heart that we would speak to Him. Don't take my word for it; take His:

*Be anxious for nothing, but in everything by prayer and supplication with thanksgiving let your requests be made known to God.*
—Philippians 4:6 NASB

*Trust in Him at all times, O people; Pour out your heart before Him; God is a refuge for us.*
—Psalm 62:8 NASB

*[P]ray without ceasing.*
—1 Thessalonians 5:17 NASB

*Pour out your heart like water before the presence of the Lord.*
—Lamentations 2:19 NASB

*Ask, and it will be given to you; seek, and you will find; knock, and it will be opened to you.*
—Matthew 7:7 NASB

His word iterates time and again how thoroughly engaged God is when we pray to Him.

In Luke 18:1, Jesus tells His disciples a parable to illustrate that they "ought always to pray and not lose heart". Jesus says, "And will not God give justice to his elect, who cry to him day and night? Will he delay long over them? I tell you, he will give justice to them speedily" (verses 7 and 8). Friends, we respond to a God who *speaks* to us first and then *hears* our prayers. This is unfathomably beautiful news. Respond to God by talking to Him. If you're new to prayer or feel incredibly uncomfortable when you attempt it, you are in good company. News flash: We all feel that way—at least at first. Honestly, *we all do*. Here's a few ways in which you can pray over God's word.

❧ *Pray over God's word by reading His word back to Him.* This is the method I used when I was first learning how to pray. I would simply read scripture back to God. I liked this method because it took all the guesswork out of praying. As I read the Bible, I found verses that resonated with me. As I prayed, I simply recited those same verses to Him. After praying this way for a while, His words slowly became my words. Here are some of the verses I used when I first began:

*I will extol you, my God and King, and bless your name forever and ever. Every day I will bless you and praise your name forever and ever.*
—Psalm 145:1–2

*Holy, holy, holy, is the Lord God Almighty, who was and is and is to come! Worthy are you, our LORD and God, to receive glory and honor and power, for you created all things, and by your will they existed and were created.*
—Revelation 4:8,11

*Have mercy on me, O God, according to your steadfast love; according to your abundant mercy blot out my transgressions.*
—Psalm 51:1

*Create in me a clean heart, O God, and renew a right spirit within me.*
—Psalm 51:10

You can also Google the phrase *prayers in the Bible* and find multiple websites that list every prayer recorded in the Bible. You can use these prayers to guide you and train you in your own prayers. That is why they are there. I have kept a copy of all of Paul's prayers in the back of my day planner for months. I often use those prayers to guide me in praying for my husband and boys. When I have no idea what to pray, I use Jesus's words in the Lord's Prayer to see me through. This method never fails.

🐦 *Pray over God's word by using the five questions.*

You can also pray by drawing on the information you find through your reading each day. Go back to your questions and consider:

Q1: What does this passage teach me about God?
For Prayer: *In light of this, how can I praise Him right now?*

Q2: What does this passage teach me about humanity?
For Prayer: *In light of this, how can I repent? What do I need to personally confess?*

Q3: What does this passage teach me about the nature of the relationship between God and humanity?
For prayer: *How has God brought restoration for me in this area? Where do I need to ask for help?*

Q4: What truth does this passage illuminate? What lie does this passage uncover?
For Prayer: *What can I thank God for? What do I need to guard against?*

Q5: What conviction, correction, instruction, encouragement, or promise does this passage offer me?
For Prayer: *Ask God to convict, correct, instruct, and encourage you through His word. Be as specific as the text allows. Ask that He would open your eyes to see His promises.*

Listening, dwelling upon, and praying over God's word are just a few ways you can engage in Step 4 of this Bible study process of responding to God's word. Much like reading God's word, responding to God's word is a discipline that takes time and commitment. Although responding to God was a completely foreign notion to me when I began studying the Bible, it is now one of the most rewarding parts of my study time. I hope you find the same to be true.

We're almost there. Come with me just a little bit further

as we take a look at the last step of this process.

## Step 5: Be changed by God's word

This last step in the process of Bible study is where the rubber meets the road. This is where the reality of everyday life crashes forcefully into the truth of God's word. This is where you experience the most friction and difficulty but also where you experience the most blessing and growth. Friends, no study of the Bible is complete if we do not allow ourselves to be changed by what we have read.

First Thessalonians 2:13 tells us that God's word effectively works in you who believe. The words within th Bible *effectively affect* us, they accomplish within us exactly what He intends to accomplish. Some of this work is very much welcomed, wanted, and eagerly anticipated. For instance, it encourages us (Rom. 15:4), it assures us (1 John 5:13), it protects us (Eph. 6:17), and it nourishes us (1 Pet. 2:2). These are things we can earnestly hope to receive when we enter into the study of God's word.

However, we must also remember that God's word is described as being "sharper than any double-edged sword" that pierces, divides, and exposes us (Heb. 4:12 NIV). I dare say we may not be quite so eager for God's word to do that kind of work. Yet this is the very work that God's word promises to do. As God's word works within us, He changes us. He makes us into a new creation (2 Cor. 5:17). When we delve into the study of His word, we must be ready to do just that: change.

As you journey through your study of scripture, you will again and again have to choose to do that hard thing the Lord is asking you to do. To forgive. To turn away from (insert harmful person, activity, or attitude here). To remember. To trust. To deny yourself. Sometimes these actions will be easy, barely a blip on the radar. At other times, they will literally bring you to your knees. That is especially when you know God's word is working. Allow yourself to be changed as God's word goes to work within you.

> *But be doers of the word, and not hearers only, deceiving yourselves.*
>
> —James 1:22

## On Questions, Misunderstandings, and Doubts

Over the course of this chapter, I have proposed a process of Bible study that should see you through from beginning to end. It's simple enough for the youngest believer to follow but has the capacity to lead even those who have studied the Bible for years to more closely perceive the depths and heights of God's word. The nature of studying anything, though, is that the more you study, the more questions you will have. That is a good thing. Questions are a sure sign that you are digging in deeply and uncovering more. Do not be afraid of them. Studying the Bible, when boiled down to its simplest form, is really nothing more than asking questions and then digging for answers. The Bible does not shy away from difficult topics. God is not reticent to speak His truth, no matter how unpopular a truth it may be. When we question from a heart that is sincerely seeking, God reveals His truth. Take a look at the compassion and transparency with which Jesus answered the questions that doubting Thomas brought forth after Jesus's resurrection:

> *Now Thomas, one of the twelve, called the Twin, was not with them when Jesus came. So the other disciples told him, "We have seen the Lord." But he said to them,*

*"Unless I see in his hands the mark of the nails, and place my finger into the mark of the nails, and place my hand into his side, I will never believe." Eight days later, his disciples were inside again, and Thomas was with them. Although the doors were locked, Jesus came and stood among them and said, "Peace be with you." Then he said to Thomas, "Put your finger here, and see my hands; and put out your hand, and place it in my side. Do not disbelieve, but believe." Thomas answered him, "My Lord and my God!"*

—John 20:24–28

How profound that Jesus's willingness to answer the doubter's question, to meet the doubter in the exact place he doubted, is the very thing that led to the doubter's belief. Each of us will surely come to places where we question, misunderstand, and, yes, even doubt, God's word. Still, if we refuse to shy away from these points of struggle and continue to press on despite our own resistance, these places of struggle can become the places of our greatest growth. Questions are good. Here are a few things you can do to approach your questions appropriately as you continue digging into God's word.

- *Enter into the question with the assumption that no matter the answer, God is right.* Because He is.

- *Use the Bible to study the Bible.* A sure way to gain greater insight into what a particular passage means is to use scripture to interpret scripture. This is called *cross-referencing*. Cross-referencing allows us to search the Bible and find other verses that reference the same themes, words, events, or people in order to gain a deeper understanding of the passage we are studying. When stuck on a difficult text, cross-referencing should be your go-to research method. Often, you will uncover the answer to your question as you read through the cross-references. Many Bibles provide you with a limited number of cross-references. I recommend biblehub.com as an excellent free resource for finding cross-references.

☙ *Always go back to context.* More than anything else, context determines the meaning of the text. It is not enough to merely know scripture. We must know it rightly. We must know it in its correct context, having a correct understanding of what it meant to its original audience. If something seems completely wrong to you as you are reading scripture, totally off base or making absolutely no sense, make sure you go back to the who, what, where, when, and why questions we discussed at the beginning of the chapter. Context is king in Bible study.

☙ *Pray, linger, and wait on the text.* Remember, we study the Bible completely dependent on God for understanding. Ask God for clarity and wisdom. Lean into the text and wait.

☙ After, and only after, you have done all this, may you consult *trusted* outside sources if you are still tripped up. There are plenty of reliable resources available at just a few clicks. It is astounding that we have such easy access to such an array of good, reliable information. However, before you feel the need to turn to outside resources every time a difficult question pops up, I want to assure you of this: There is no need to feel such an urgency.

## You + the Holy Spirit + the Bible = everything you need to understand the Bible

If you had not even one additional resource available to you, you could *still* absolutely come to understand the Bible. As my friend Kristina pointed out, a woman living in the depths of a jungle with nothing but a Bible in her hand can know the Lord just as closely as those like you and me who have an abundance of resources at hand.

As wonderful as these resources are, there is no way to overturn every Bible study stone as you're working your way book by book through the Bible. Go ahead and follow the occasional rabbit trail when something from the text grabs your attention, but be sure to return to the task at hand. Keep working your way through the book to which you have committed. On more than one occasion, I have stumbled across a verse in my daily reading that all of a sudden illuminated a question I had long held. These moments are worth the wait. They are when you hear God speaking specifically to you so clearly. Don't rush so forcefully into understanding that you miss the blessing of the wait.

*For the* LORD *gives wisdom; from his mouth come knowledge and understanding.*
—Proverbs 2:6

That's it. We made it! And there you have a five-step process to guide your independent study of the Bible.

Step 1: Pick a book of the Bible.

Step 2:  Study the context of the book.

Step 3:  Read the book.

Step 4:  Respond to God's word.

Step 5:  Be changed by God's word.

As you reflect on the incredible amount of information we've covered in this chapter, please keep in mind that *you will never take all five steps in any one sitting.* It will break down for you something like this:

**Step 1:** Put time and prayer into this step. No need to rush here. Take a few days (or longer) to decide what book you want to read. After that, this step is over. You don't have to repeat it until you begin a new book.

**Step 2:** This will take up only a day or two of study. I already told you where you could find all the answers. After that, Step 2 is over. You don't have to repeat it until you begin a new book.

**Step 3:** This is where your everyday work comes in. The good news is that after your first read-through of the book, which might take a few days or weeks, you move at the pace of only one chapter a day. This is so doable. As a point of reference, my Bible study buddies, Julie and Brenna, both clocked in about 15–20 minutes to complete one chapter of reading and the five questions for that chapter. If one chapter a day isn't doable for you (I have been there), then break it up even more. The point here is for you to keep on keeping on. Keep reading. Keep answering those five questions. Keep making progress.

**Step 4:** Like Step 3, Step 4 also requires daily work. Respond to what God has spoken to you each and every day, but bear in mind that there is no time requirement here. Silence any attempts your inner legalist self makes to count minutes. Respond in ways you enjoy and come naturally to you. Steps 3 and 4 can even occur simultaneously as you read and respond, and then read a bit further and respond some more.

**Step 5:** This step will flow through an increasing knowledge of God and His word. It is more a result that God brings about in you as you study His word than a step you set out to complete for yourself.

You can totally do this. You have the tools you need in hand. Now pick up the spoon and eat.

> *Like newborn infants, long for the pure spiritual milk,*
> *that by it you may grow up into salvation—if indeed*
> *you have tasted that the Lord is good.*
>
> —1 Peter 2:2–3

## Chapter 8: On Babies and Bathwater: Some Thoughts on Returning to the Bible Study

*Let the word of Christ dwell in you richly, teaching and admonishing one another in all wisdom, singing psalms and hymns and spiritual songs, with thankfulness in your hearts to God.*

—Colossians 3:16

In August 2010, my husband and I began a Bible study class alongside 11 other couples at the big Baptist church we attended at the time. For three and a half years, we met with those same people (and the others that followed) every Sunday morning to study God's word. The years we spent with those couples, studying and teaching the Bible and growing in community, were some of the most fruitful years of my Christian walk so far. I could see so clearly how each person fit, the gifts God had given them, and the way their gifts served the community. Christ designed us to work together in this way. There is great value in recognizing and deferring to the gifting of others in the body of Christ, but never to the extent that we neglect our own relationship with God and His word in the process. While some may be particularly good at intercessory prayer and others at service or teaching, we were all designed to be good at the Bible.

I began this book by beckoning you away from the ever-popular Bible study approach to an independent study of God's word. I suppose that in many ways, this book is a response to the trend I have noticed for people (especially women) to flock to organized group Bible studies and yet shrink back from their individual study of God's word. Although I was careful in the introduction to make my stance on Bible studies clear, at this point I feel like I might need to do that again. I'm not at all suggesting we do away with Bible studies and Bible study resources. These events, gatherings, and resources are some of the many benefits of being part of the body of believers. In no way am I suggesting that we do away with them. Women's Bible studies are one of my favorite things on earth. If you want to see me completely geek out, just throw me in a room full of women who have Bibles in their laps and pens in their hands. Corporate worship, study, and fellowship are encouraged in the Bible. They are very good things. In describing the early Christian church, Luke writes:

> *And they devoted themselves to the apostles' teaching and the fellowship, to the breaking of bread and the prayers.*
>
> —Acts 2:42

This is a description of what the early church was like, and it is prescriptive of what we, too, should do as believers today. Let us do all these things, but may they bolster, inform, and further our love and understanding of God's word, *not replace our own study of it*. That being said, I want to end this book with some suggestions on how to do pre-written or group Bible studies well. After all, there is no need to throw out the baby with the bathwater. My aim in this last chapter is to answer this question: How do we do Bible study well when we do Bible study together?

## How to Do Bible Studies Well

A portion of this burden necessarily falls on the shoulders of the teachers, writers, pastors, and ministry leaders who produce and/or choose materials for Bible study purposes. Those of us who take on these roles must intentionally consider two factors when it comes to placing Bible studies before the people of our church. The first has to do with the content of the Bible study; the second has to do with the process of the Bible study. Let's first turn our attention to content.

### Content of our Bible studies

There are entire bookstores devoted to Bible studies and related resources. Here in the suburbs of Houston, Texas, these bookstores are easy to come by. Walk into any one of them and there is a mind-boggling number of studies from which to choose. Given the overwhelming amount of Bible study material available, how do we know which one to choose? Here are a few questions for you to consider.

1. **Is it a good Bible study?** All Bible studies are not created equal. Here are some characteristics I have noticed that mark a good Bible study.

> ✒ *A good Bible study requires the learner to actually be in the Bible.* That means physically navigating through its thin, flimsy pages with your own two hands. I became a Christian relatively later in life, so I didn't have the benefit of any type of training in my formative years to help me learn my way around the Bible. In the beginning, part of my apprehension about studying the Bible was that I couldn't even navigate it. If you had asked me where the book of Hebrews was, my best guess would have been somewhere in

the Old Testament. (I mean, it kind of sounds Old Testament-y, doesn't it?) It took me years of flipping through the pages of the Bible as I read, studied, and looked up verses for me to feel comfortable and confident enough to navigate it on my own. This type of confidence is an invaluable resource when it comes to studying the Bible. A good Bible study should make the Bible physically more familiar to the learner. That requires the study to be grounded by and rooted in Biblical text.

- *A good Bible study keeps the focus of the Bible as the focus of the study.* The point of the Bible is God. Every book, every story, every character, and every event in the Bible reveals information regarding the nature and character of God. The Bible is *not* a book about us, and it should not be treated as if it is. Yes, we will discover truths about who we are as we study the Bible, but that should not be the primary purpose of Bible study. We study the Bible to learn about God.

- *A good Bible study keeps the big picture narrative of the Bible in view.* The Bible tells the most epic story of all time. Understanding the big picture of this one story is crucial to accurately understanding each individual character, book, story, or event in the Bible. A good Bible study illuminates for the learner how the specific area of focus for any particular study fits into the whole of scripture—into the big story of the Bible. In this way, a good Bible study goes beyond itself. No Bible study should terminate on itself but should thrust learners deeper into the pages of scripture and entrench them in the narrative that spans the entire Bible.

✍ *A good Bible study addresses the interconnectedness of the Old and New Testaments.* To a large extent, this characteristic goes hand in hand with the previous one about the importance of the Biblical narrative. Because the Bible tells *one* story, we must be diligent in pointing out how the two Testaments inform each other.

For instance, although the Old Testament never mentions Jesus by name, Jesus Himself proclaimed that the Old Testament was about Him (Luke 24:25–27). So in order to be taught accurately, a study of any Old Testament book, character, theme, or event should be inundated with Jesus. Conversely, the New Testament contains hundreds of direct citations from the Old Testament. Its writers continually point back to Old Testament themes, characters, laws, and events. A good study of the New Testament will take the time to explain why. Why does Paul discuss Abraham at such great length in the books of Romans and Galatians? Why does Jesus read a scroll from the book of Isaiah (Luke 4:17)? What is Philip referring to when he says he found the one of whom Moses wrote (John 1:45)?

A good Bible study will tackle the interdependence of the Old and New Testaments head on, as it teaches learners to use the Bible to study the Bible.

✍ *Finally, a good Bible study encourages and equips learners to study the Bible on their own.* If the study you're considering does all of the above well, chances are it's already doing this well, too. When a Bible study familiarizes the student with the Bible, constantly keeps itself oriented toward the main character of the Bible (God), and expands the student's understanding of the entire Biblical narrative, the student is learning foundational Bible study principles that will transition into an independent study time.

In fact, that is exactly how I learned how to study the Bible—by listening to and reading material from teachers who taught the Bible well. I learned to imitate their study habits and make them my own. A good Bible study emphasizes and teaches process by carrying an awareness that learners will pick up on the study techniques used in those studies. Learners will notice the questions that a good Bible study asks about a text and then will learn to ask those questions for themselves. Learners will notice how a good Bible study uses the New Testament to explain the Old Testament and then look for places in their independent study where they can do that. Learners will notice the reoccurring themes and topics within a good Bible study and begin to search for those elsewhere in scripture. A good Bible study is not content with merely teaching the Bible but also strives to teach Bible students how to effectively study the Bible so they can behold the wonders of God's living word for themselves.

Even using the above criteria to narrow your search, there is still an abundance of good Bible studies to place before the people of our churches. In addition to asking if it's a *good* Bible study, we must also ask if it's the *right* Bible study.

**2. Is it the right Bible study for this group for this time in our church?** You've found a good Bible study, but is it the right Bible study for your specific group right now? For years, my understanding of the Bible was fragmented, not because I *wasn't* studying the Bible, but because there was no rhyme or reason to what I was studying. I would jump from study to study without giving any thought to how one study informed the next. My learning, although consistent, was disjointed. Through this piecemeal approach to Bible study, I learned a lot about biblical principles, but I could not properly place them within the context of the biblical narrative—which is where the heart of the Bible lies.

For instance, you may understand the principle of the Ten Commandments, but without understanding the heart of the Father in giving those commandments, you've missed the point of the principle and done little to promote your understanding of the character of God or the Bible as a whole. In order to produce this type of whole-Bible understanding, we want to draw clear connections about how the particular study chosen for any particular group Bible study fits in with what the church is walking through on Sunday mornings. We shouldn't pick a Bible study until we have asked, "How does this study complement/inform/shed light on what's being taught on Sunday mornings?" Because the Bible is one, unified story, chances are there *is* a sound answer to that question, but if you can't answer it, the people in your Bible study group won't be able to either.

## Process of our Bible Studies

Another factor we must consider in doing Bible study well is the *process* of our Bible study. By that I mean, how do we come together and *do* Bible study well? What does that look like? How do we make the most of the relatively short time we have together? I've been part of my fair share of group Bible studies over the years, and I've taken note of characteristics that distinguish a good group Bible study from a merely well-intentioned group Bible study.

**1. The good group Bible study listens to God's word as it speaks.** The first assumption we must carry with us into any Bible study is that God's word speaks. More pointedly, we must assume that God speaks to us through His word, exactly where we are—no matter where that may be. Most of you reading this probably believe this is true, but do we run our group Bible studies as if this is, in fact, the truth? Do we allow God's word to be the focal point, the gathering place, and the main event of our group studies? Or do we allow relationship building and small talk to take center stage? Women are generally good talkers; we seem to be innately wired for connecting with each other in this way. This type of connection is a good and worthy pursuit that has its place in women's ministry and can even be appropriately built in to group study time. However, in our group studies we want to intentionally put our main focus on listening rather than talking. Yes, we want to listen to each other—to hear the needs and prayers of our fellow sojourners—but more than that, we want to listen to God.

A good group Bible study will focus intently on listening to God's word so we might hear what He is saying to us. To do this, we must unapologetically push other things aside in order to spend time in the Bible— reading His word and listening to His word being taught to us. We must trust that His word contains more wisdom, help, and healing than any words we may want to speak. When we do this, we are instilling within the women under our leadership the same confidence—that God's word speaks directly to us. Second Timothy 3:16–17 tells us, "All Scripture is breathed out by God and profitable for teaching, for reproof, for correction, and for training in righteousness, that the man of God may be complete, equipped for every good work."

The Bible contains everything we need to know in order to be saved and to follow Christ with our lives. Peter puts it quite bluntly, "His divine power has granted to us all things that pertain to life" (2 Pet. 1:3). That means that whatever answer someone may be searching for, it's there. Trusting this frees us up with respect to our fellow Christians. We don't have to bend over backward trying to figure out every woman's problems or ease all her pain. We merely need to provide her with the time and the environment in which she can learn to hear God's answer for herself.

**2. The good group Bible study allows God's word do its work.** In chapter 7, we saw that being changed by God's word is a necessary part of the Bible study process. The apostle Paul tells us that God's word is at work in those who believe (1 Thess. 2:13). God's word seeks to affect us and effect change in us. Some of this will feel good and be very much wanted. We will be encouraged, assured, protected, and nourished through His word. However, we must also remember that God's word is described as being "sharper than any double-edged sword" that pierces, divides, and exposes us, as we saw previously (Heb. 4:12 NIV).

In the group setting, it is imperative that we learn to recognize the work of God's word so we can get out of its way. That allows the word to do what it purposes to do with both the comforting and convicting edges of that sword. When Peter shared the gospel at Pentecost, those listening were "cut to the heart" and came under deep conviction (Acts 2:37). Peter, responding rightly to the work of God's word, did not protect them from this conviction but echoed it, instructing the hearers, "Repent and be baptized every one of you in the name of Jesus Christ for the forgiveness of your sins" (Acts 2:38). Likewise, as teachers and leaders of group Bible studies, we must allow God's word to "cut both ways" as I heard Nancy Guthrie once say it. We must allow God's word to not only comfort women but to convict them. This is part of the hard work of a good group Bible study—the relentless chasing after the *whole* of God's work through His word.

**3. The good group Bible study holds tightly to truth as it guards against speculation.** The portion of group study time that is most susceptible to sliding the slippery slope from truth to speculation is the small-group discussion time. Even the best group Bible study can derail during this time if the discussion is not well led or properly managed. From a learner's perspective, I have found the group discussion session to be either the most fruitful and rewarding part of the study or the most distracting and disorienting part, depending on the ability of the leader to guard against unfounded speculation within her group. Here are some pitfalls leaders want to avoid in order to guard against unfounded speculation within a small group.

> *In group discussion, we want to be careful that we don't force application.* I have a strong conviction that the entirety of God's word is immediately applicable to each and every one of us. However, that doesn't always end up looking like the application many people expect when coming to a Bible study. The application portion of Bible study can't always be boiled down to a couple of action steps, and we must not give in to the notion that it can. When we force application, we may be unwittingly bypassing the most important work of the Bible—to draw us closer to God. We must resist the temptation to make things applicable by asking *What do I need to do for myself now?* when the actual point of the study is to more accurately understand what

God has done through Christ on our behalf. More often than not, I have found God's word to be most immediately applicable when I come to know more about God—His nature, His character, or perhaps even His promises. Our take aways from Bible study will more likely be what God revealed *about Himself* to us than what God has revealed about our lives, our problems, our questions, or our fears. When we have a more accurate understanding of who God is, it brings all those other things into greater focus.

❧ *In group discussion, we want to avoid the emphasis on our own thoughts and feelings.* Hopefully, we will enter into any Bible study having carefully considered the text at hand, and come armed with lots of thoughts of our own regarding the passages covered. However, ultimately, we must acknowledge that *our thoughts about the Bible are not as important as thinking rightly about the Bible.* That is to say, we must be prepared to submit our thoughts and feelings on any given portion of scripture to the truth of God's word. Instead of chasing our tails, discussing hypothetical possibilities of what a portion of scripture does or does not mean, we must do the hard work of studying scripture in light of scripture. That means that the best Bible study tool is the Bible itself.

When discussing what a portion of scripture means, we should not focus on our own thoughts and feelings about that text, but instead focus on what God meant by giving us that text. We figure this out by examining it within the context of the whole biblical narrative. We also use other portions of scripture that teach on similar topics to further our understanding of a text or biblical concept. After all, who better than the author of a book to tell us what is meant by that book? Isaiah 55:9 reminds us that God's ways are higher than our ways and His thoughts higher than our thoughts. We cannot arrogantly enter into Bible study assuming that our thoughts and feelings about God's word determine truth, but must humbly posture our hearts before God and pray for a heart willing to accept the truth offered.

🪶 *In group discussion, we want to avoid filtering God's word through our lives.* Rather we should encourage each other to filter *our lives* through *His word.* This practice anchors our lives and our study of the Bible to the truth of God's word instead of our ever-changing and constantly shifting circumstances. Because Jesus Christ is the same yesterday, today, and forever (Heb. 13:8), He—the *living* Word—is able to offer us stability no matter how off-kilter our lives may currently seem.

As teachers and leaders of group Bible study, we echo Paul's sentiment to the church at Corinth when he wrote:

*Follow my example, as I follow the example of Christ.*
—1 Corinthians 11:1 NIV

We follow Christ in word and in deed, but also through our unabashed dependence on scripture. If we treat scripture as if it is able and sufficient to meet each of us where we are, those under our leadership and teaching will learn to treat it as such, too. In short, we encourage dependence on God's word by modeling it.

I have personally found women's group Bible studies to be one of the most enjoyable aspects of belonging to the body of Christ. I have made some of my dearest friends in these settings, several of whom worked alongside me in getting this book to you. Ideally, these group studies give us a place to safely ask questions, learn from those who have walked with the Lord longer than we have, and build one another up. Group studies are a beautiful way that individuals within the church can grow in their faith and knowledge of God. We can do group Bible study well by picking the right content at the right time for the people of our church and by keeping a close watch on the process of our study time together. May our group study time serve to further embolden each of us to dig into God's word with our very own hands.

# Conclusion
# Pick Up Your Bible

As I've gone about living life these past 37 years, I've set my heart intently on finding a number of different things from a number of different places. I've chased after success, acceptance, love, and happiness. I've run hard after comfort, stability, achievement, and security. Some of these things I've found, although a few continue to elude me. But of those that I *have* managed to find, each has ultimately disappointed me in one way or another and ended up being just a bit less than what I had hoped. While loving and being loved most certainly delivers all the highs I had imagined, it also comes with lows that are difficult to fathom. Stability grounds me for a stretch but then leaves me longing for just a bit more excitement. Achievement is quickly trumped by the need to do just a bit more, be just a bit better. At the end of each day, all my seeking and finding still left something to be desired. *And then I set my heart intently on finding God through His word.* This pursuit alone has not disappointed.

I don't know where each of you are in your pursuit of the Lord right now. I wish I could pull up a chair and sit across from you a while. I wish I could see your face and hear your story, listen to where you are and where you've been, and know how you have perceived God to be active (or inactive) in and through all of it. I know that as life goes on, we all fall and fail and get busted up something fierce. I also know that in the midst of all the trials and troubles and heartbreak of living, we sometimes begin to believe the lie that God is far off, distant, unconcerned, or silent. But that is so far from the truth. God is speaking. To *you*. Right now. His voice rings clear in each and every page of scripture. My encouragement to you today is to pick up your Bible and read. Lean into scripture and listen intently for His voice. The duty of independent interaction with God's word will always come to rest on the shoulders of each of us individually. Friends, *we must not be too timid or apathetic to grab hold of God's word with our own two hands.* Having received faith, let us continue in it (Col. 2:6–7), paying close attention to what we've heard so we do not drift away (Heb. 2:1–4). May we dare not neglect our salvation since each one of us will one day give an account—you for you and me for me (Heb. 4:13).

God's word is infinitely more worthy than any of the libraries of words written about His word. There comes a point when every Bible study girl needs to sit down with nothing but her Bible. No pastor, teacher, or other intermediary. Just a girl and her Bible. This type of intimate meeting with the Lord through His word produces a level of knowledge of Him that can be obtained through no other means. It is not only *beneficial* to study God's word in this way, it is *necessary*, a responsibility God has placed upon each and every believer. Pick up your Bible. He'll meet you there.

> *But from there you will seek the Lord your God and you will find him, if you search after him with all your heart and with all your soul.*
>
> —Deuteronomy 4:29

**Coming Soon**

Study the Bible book-by-book using
*His Word Alone* companion study guides.
Follow the His Word Alone website for availability.

For content, downloads, and resources, please visit
www.hiswordalone.com/book.

CPSIA information can be obtained
at www.ICGtesting.com
Printed in the USA
FSHW01n0810280718
50741FS